Series - Book 1

Again, God Speaks!

God Reveals His Hidden Secrets
Genesis 2:7-8

John F. Boylan, M. Div.

© January 2011

Copyright © 2011 by John F. Boylan, M.Div.
U.S. Copyright Office
TXu 1- 763- 207
Library Of Congress Cataloging - Publication Data Pending

ISBN: 978-0-578-09117-4

Publisher: Day Spring Institute
Richardson, Texas 75080

Table of Contents

Acknowledgements 4

Introduction 5

Chapter 1 - Will You Listen If God Speaks to You? 8

Chapter 2 - The Name 'Jesus' Revealed
In Genesis 2:7-8 13

Chapter 3 - First Things First – The
Story Itself 20

Chapter 4 - The Existence of God Proven
By Science 28

Chapter 5 - Yahweh and Yeshua A
Paradoxical Unity 38

Chapter 6 - The Clue 53

Chapter 7 - Consubstantial Relationship
Of the Son 63

Chapter 8 - So What Do I Do Now 106

Chapter 9 – Types of Encryptions Found
In This Study 116

Epilogue 127

Appendix i - Not Bible Codes 129

Appendix ii - Is the Hebrew Name For
Jesus - Yeshua ישוע or Yeshu ישו? 140

Bibliography 144

Acknowledgements

Many people have encouraged me in this study but foremost is my wife Teresa. She above all others has kept this work moving and heading toward publication. She is the heart of this project. I am truly amazed that she never lost sight of God's Hand at work in this study even when I could not see beyond the minutia. She pushed me and prodded, she encouraged me and cajoled. She prayed and somehow God's revelations emerged from it all.

A major debt of gratitude goes to Joel Young and Yacov Rambsel who began the research into ELS patterns revealing Yeshua's Name long before I even knew of such things. They opened the door I entered in and quickly realized there was so much more in the text than simple ELS patterns. The Holy Spirit took over from there by igniting my interest and directly providing the revelations which you are about to see in this book.

I also thank the Fulton Family, Tom, Susan and especially Eric – for their loving support and interest, the Randy Glen family for their support and wonderful encouragement, Sarah Arion who patiently read the early editions of this text - her amazement at what was obviously in front of her told me 'truly this is from God', David and Janice Sapp, Tony and Carrie Justice who too were amazed at what was unfolding in front of them, thanks and prayers for you too. Without knowing it, all of you *were there* when I wanted to give up. This is true. You 'were there' when it was dark and when I was discouraged. I know God sent you to encourage me and I pray that His blessings to be with you always.

I thank and glorify my God Who is the Faithful and True Author of all the reader is about to see. I thank Him that He has allowed me, to play this small part in His eternal revelation which is ongoing yet determined, ever emerging yet eternally the same. May He be glorified and may His Name be glorified, always and in all things.   John Boylan

Introduction

Why Has God Hidden So Much Christian Teaching Into The Jewish Text Of The Creation Story?

As obvious as it may seem, the reason why God has hidden so much Christian teaching into the text of the story of the creation of humankind is that He wants us, today, in this time in history, to once again pay attention to His teachings. This is an age which has been referred to as being a Godless age and an age characterized by a lack of faith and piety. Indeed, never before in the history of the world has there been such a monumental falling away from belief as we see occurring at this moment in time. It has been said in the past, when Messiah comes will He find faith upon the earth? The answer to this question is probably no. That is, the answer is no…, unless…, unless that is, God Himself intervenes and once more advents into the creation and once again teaches us what He would have us believe.

He did this once before thousands of years ago, during the wilderness journey of the Jewish people. The setting was the rugged outcropping of Mount Sinai where He dictated, according to tradition, 'letter by letter' the entirety of the first five books in the Bible i.e., the Torah.

Today, He is once again revealing His Presence to a generation desperately in need of a Savior. This He is doing by bringing into the light of day Hidden teachings which He encrypted into the text of the Bible many thousands of years ago. These Newly revealed teachings confirm what has historically been taught about One remarkable Being, Yeshua the Messiah Who is also known as Jesus, the Christ of Israel.

This book is challenging to people who do not accept Jesus as being the 'Christ of Israel'. It can be especially challenging to Jewish faithful everywhere who reject Jesus categorically. Nevertheless, such ones will be hard pressed to explain how clear Yeshuan i.e., Christian, teaching has been so amazingly embedded into the text of their sacred scriptures - especially the Torah.

Jewish faithful refer to the first five books of the Old Testament as 'the Torah' - תורה. The word Torah means 'teaching' i.e., God's teaching.[1] Because it is also believed that the Torah was dictated by God to Moses 'letter by letter' it is, understandably, treated by the faithful with the utmost respect and honor. The Jews revere each word, each phrase and each letter. Many attend special schools where the main subject studied is the Torah. It is safe to say the end product of such devotedness is the formation of a believer who 'eats, drinks and breaths' the text of the Torah.

For this reason, the Jewish faith has steadfastly mandated that not one letter may be omitted or added - from or to - the text as new Torah copies are made. This dynamic has accounted for the near flawless transmission of the Torah text over the vast millennia of time encompassing Jewish history.

What the reader will find utterly astounding as he reads through this book is the fact that it is precisely this 'flawless transmission of the Jewish text' which has also resulted in the preservation of an enormous volume of Christian teaching which has been encrypted[2] into the two short verses under consideration in this book, namely, Genesis 2:7-8. The question which should be prompted by this observation is this: "*How* did so much 'Christian' material get into these 103 letters of Hebrew text in the first place?"

Hopefully, by the time you are finished reading this book, the answer will be evident to you. The answer is, God Himself placed it there.

Obviously, this is an extremely bold assertion; still, it is proven by God's manner of encrypting this material so

---

[1] The word "Torah" in Hebrew "is derived from the root ירה which in the hifil conjugation means "to teach" (cf. Lev. 10:11) Wikipedia, Torah.
[2] See Chapter 8 - Types of Encryption Found in this study

stunningly, so clearly, that any other conclusion than this conclusion is just simply…, well…, it's just simply silly.

It can now be said:

'herein is contained the first purely, objective and verifiable proof' that God exists and that He has a Begotten Son, Whom we know by the Name Yeshua, i.e., Jesus.'

How To Read This Book

In a word, 'slowly'. There is a considerable amount of sacred teaching contained in its pages, revelations direct from Yahweh Elohim – God. Pay particular attention to the illustrations of the Hebrew text; try to 'connect the dots' as you read the commentaries. Understand as you do this, *the 'commentaries are not the revelations.* Commentary is not what this book is about. It is *exclusively about God's revelations* and God's revelations are visible only in the illustrations. Enjoy your study. You are about to see, 'that which eye has never seen before!

JB

Chapter 1 - Will You Listen If God Speaks to You?

This book is different than any other book which you have ever read. This is because the primary subject matter upon which it focuses was not written by the author whose name appears on its cover. Rather, the 'content of interest' which is but merely presented by its author, was in fact, written by God Himself! For example, one such mystery is *'the God encrypted'* Hebrew Name for Jesus i.e., Yeshua, which He deeply embedded into the story of the creation. Incredible!

Truly, this book is about the eternal mysteries of God, the eternal 'hidden mysteries' of God, which He is now revealing in our sight today. Moreover, in the revelation of these mysteries today, we come to understand God's eternal love for us in a way that is truly different than what we may have experienced before. Instead of 'learning the fact' that God loves us or memorizing Bible verses which testify to this fact or studying religious doctrine which points to this teaching, this book enables all of us to directly observe and experience the Father's love and concern for us in our recognition that His encrypted revelations are His invitation to us to return into Holy Fellowship with Him, a fellowship breached by the sin of man. He is also, once more, revealing to us today, the 'Holy Provision' He has made to bring about this greatly to be desired reconciliation; and in this, He is inviting us, at this very moment, to accept His Provision and thus-by enter into the gentle rest of unity with Him, the embrace of our Heavenly and All-Holy Father and God.

Amazingly, God has chosen to emerge from the 'apparent silence' of millennia to once more lovingly interact with His creation; and, He has chosen to do so at this precise moment in time. He has chosen this time and this method of revelation to once more affirm to an estranged generation that He is God, the God Who delivers all men from the consequences of sin and its enslaving potential upon our creaturely natures. This is a time when God is once more, by way of direct revelation, reaffirming His ancient teachings regarding Himself and His Beloved Messiah. This is a time when God is once more calling out to each of us to reconsider his or her life and to return to Him, embracing Him as our loving Father. This is a time when God is giving each of us *one last chance* to be restored to Him *before He acts*.

Hence, this is also a time of dire warning and joyful anticipation. Messiah is about to explode upon and into the creation, declaring the Kingdom of the Father, lovingly receiving all who will accept His invitation to become its citizens and broken-heartedly destroying all who will persist in wayward rebellion.

Ancient Teachings Reaffirmed Today

God's hidden mysteries, discussed in this book, are as ancient as the Old Testament itself. They are as ancient as the activity of the Lord God dictating to Moses, letter by letter, the Holy Torah, the first 5 books of the Old Testament, namely, Genesis, Exodus, Leviticus, Numbers and Deuteronomy. Indeed, these mysteries are as ancient as Eden and its sacred garden, the 'Garden of Paradise'. The dictation just mentioned was given by God to Moses for the Israelites, the Jewish Nation – His Chosen People. Therefore, these five books are today very sacred to the Jewish people exactly as they have been sacred throughout the ages. They are sacred to Christians also since Christians are the people who were grafted i.e., joined, into the symbolic 'olive tree', Israel; and by this blessing alone, the gentile nations share in the saving purpose, love, and redemption of God's Messiah.

Background

We will begin with some background information about the 22 letters of the Hebrew alphabet found on the front cover and throughout this book. This is because, God has chosen to reveal Himself and His Mysteries through the layout and arrangement of the *very letters* which comprise

9

the text of the Bible. Traditionally, these Hebrew letters are considered astoundingly Holy, so Holy that a person who is commissioned to copy a Hebrew Torah scroll, for example, is charged to make no error whatsoever. In fact, if an error is made, the entire scroll in progress would be discarded! Therefore, the copying of a new scroll is a great responsibility as it cannot be changed, or corrected. A new page cannot simply be added into the original work replacing the page containing the error. Again, this is considered a grave, strict, and awesome undertaking by the Jewish scholar or Rabbi. When Jewish students study the Torah, they are studying with a high level of certainty that what they are studying is the original Torah that Yahweh dictated to Moses!

Indeed, these letters are truly sacred. First of all, they represent utterances from the mouth of God Himself. They are God breathed. Secondly, we can now see, that it is through them i.e., what they reveal in terms of teaching, that the pathway back to the Father, to our eternal home, can now be powerfully and irrefutably presented, to even the most skeptical of non-believer.

Why This Book Is So Important

Most of us have had many teachers in our lives; but now, dear reader, your teacher is 'God Himself', the Almighty One, the Sovereign Lord and Creator of All Things. Marvel at this fact. Marvel at it!

God, as our Teacher, is directly, Personally, teaching us exact truths about Himself. He Himself ends the need for debate and speculation. He reduces theology to just one question, 'do we accept His teaching or not'.

"Again, God Speaks, God Reveals His Hidden Secrets, Genesis 2:7-8", *is God's Own present time revelation in His Own write* to us, His creatures. Be assured, whether you are a theologian, learner, beginner, Jew, Christian, or of any other belief, or of no belief whatsoever, there are a multitude of surprising discoveries that await you in these pages.

Perhaps you have been turned off of faith in God for reasons dealing with church abuse by church hierarchy, or churches proclaiming to be the True Church but producing nothing but empty or 'spoiled fruits'. Perhaps you are one of many thousands of people who are confused by the many changes in your church or faith, including those faiths that have gravitated toward the World Council of Churches. Perhaps you are even sick at heart or have fallen away from your faith from, the so-called, 'religious people' who are the "white-washed tombs" spoken about by Yeshua, Jesus, the ones, He says, "who are beautiful on the outside but inside they are filled with corruption and dead men's bones".

> 'Woe to you, Scribes and Pharisees, hypocrites! because ye are like to whitewashed sepulchers, which outwardly indeed do appear beautiful, and within are full of bones of dead men, and of all corruption. Matt.23:27

Perhaps you are faint-hearted or depressed because God seems nowhere to be found in a world that increasingly becomes more evil every day. Perhaps you feel alone or are plagued by drug, alcohol, or any variety of satanic addictions. Perhaps you have lost a loved one, your home, your job, or your marriage, child or spouse. Or, maybe you find yourself in the state of contentment and happiness but feel that something truly important is just missing from your life.

Whatever place you find yourself in today, be assured that your life will radically change after what you will encounter in this book; namely, that God, the Lover of Mankind Himself instructs and directs your study today. Our wanderings in desert places have now come to an end! Be mindful that Our Lord has waited until now, in these confusing, evil, and very last days to present once more His precious truths for us. Will you choose to listen to Him now, as Again, God Speaks? Will you choose to listen now, as this time God Himself speaks directly to you? Because:…,

If you will not listen to the eternal God Himself, who will you listen to?

Chapter 2 - The Name 'Jesus' Revealed in Genesis 2:7-8

As you observe the revelations brought out in the illustrations of the Hebrew box aligned text of Genesis 2:7-8, (illustrated below) it should be asked, in fact, it must be asked,

Why would God Who dictated His scripture to His servant Moses 'letter by painstaking letter'[3], do so in such a way, that with nothing more than a simple 'box alignment' of the text, the name Yeshua - יֵשׁוּעַ, Jesus, instantly becomes clearly visible, almost jumping right off the page in the sight of even the most skeptical observer?

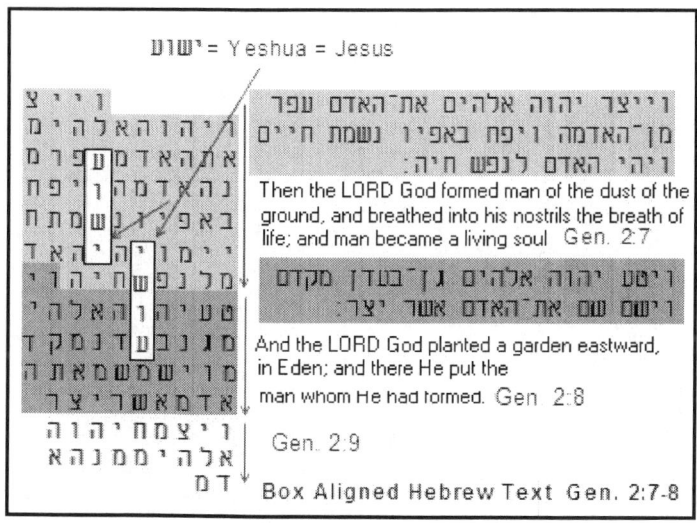

Shocked? You should be shocked!

It is shocking because, here is the Name 'Jesus' i.e., Yeshua, stunningly revealed in the Biblical text. It is the very Name of the very Being Who is said to be the **Creator**

---

[3] Jewish teaching asserts God dictated this text to Moses 'letter by painstaking letter'

Himself; and, His Name is centered within the very story in which it is said He was the Primary Participant; namely, the act of His creating mankind!

The answer to this question is hinted at in the writings of the prophet Isaiah:

"I will give thee treasures of darkness, and the hidden riches of secret places." Is. 45:3
"See all this; and will thou not declare it? ..., even hidden things, and thou didst not know them. Is. 48:6

The reason, offered by Isaiah is this:

'The Creator', left so very many Christian focused revelations in the Creation story because He wants us to discover them and declare them – at this time – at this point in history! Amazingly, *each and every one* of these 'Creator encrypted revelations' directly reveals some aspect of the Divinity, the Humanity or the Messiahship of..., Himself!

A Comment
I started this book off by displaying this incredible 'decrypted revelation' which twice spells the Name of Yeshua, Jesus. I did this in the hope of *getting the readers attention and earning readership credibility* because the following statement is so 'in-credible' that although it is absolutely true, it is nevertheless hard to believe.

There are a total of 35 additional, equally remarkable, revelations encrypted into the exact same 103 letters of Genesis 2:7-8.

The List
Here is the list of the 35 additional revelations, *'the hidden things (which) thou didst not know'* encrypted into the seemingly simple story of Gen. 2:7-8. These teachings

are amazingly embedded into the texts under review in a remarkably wide variety of encrypted patterns. Please keep in mind as you read through the book, these revealed encryptions are as old as the Bible itself and were put there by the Author of that Divine text. They have been hidden, undisclosed, until now. We need to develop a sense of reverence as we read them today. They are God's Own teaching, they are His Torah. Truly, God is revealing Himself to each of us. As you read this book please keep this list handy, refer to it often, and use it as a reference for your study and reflection.

The Divinity of Yeshua i.e., Jesus
1. Yahweh and Yeshua are One
2. Yahweh and Yeshua are both Unique
3. Yeshua is God
4. Yeshua is revealed to be the 'I Am', i.e., God
5. Yeshua is revealed to be the *'Creating Word'* of God i.e., the Word of God
6. Yeshua is revealed to be the 'HaShem'[4]
7. Yeshua is revealed to be 'the paradoxical latent presence of change within the changeless'
8. Yeshua is referred to as, the Only Begotten Son of God
9. Yeshua, is revealed to be consubstantial[5] with Yahweh Elohim
10. Yeshua is revealed to be proceeding forth from Yahweh Elohim and receding back into Yahweh Elohim[6]
11. Yeshua is referred to as 'God revealed'
12. Yeshua is revealed to be the very 'condition of existence itself'

---

[4] The phrase HaShem is a substitute Name for God. Jewish faithful say HaShem (meaning The Name) rather than running the risk of pronouncing any of God's Names in a disrespectful manner.
[5] Of 'one substance' i.e., in this case, the Divine substance
[6] Per the Nicene Creed

13. Yeshua's dual 'origination' revealed, He is God the Word and God the Son, perfect God and perfect Man
14. God's Begotten Son, is revealed to have taken on the form of Yeshua
15. God's Begotten Son, Yeshua, is revealed to have taken on the form of a servant
16. God's Begotten Son, Yeshua, is revealed to have become man and shed His blood upon the cross

The Humanity of Yeshua
17. Yeshua is revealed to have a 'human Mother
18. Yeshua's mothers name revealed: it is Mary, Miriam.
19. Yeshua is revealed to have been nursed as a human baby – thus affirming His full human nature

The Messiahship of Yeshua
20. As prophesized, the Word of God, Yeshua, is revealed to have existed before the foundations of the creation itself[7]
21. As prophesized, Yeshua is revealed to be of the lineage of Jesse
22. As prophesized, Yeshua is revealed to be of the house of Judah
23. As prophesized, Yeshua is the 'bond servant' – taking upon Himself the form of a servant
24. As prophesized, Yeshua is referred to as the 'Righteous Branch' spoken of by the prophets
25. As prophesized, Yeshua is revealed to be the 'Kinsman Redeemer'
26. As prophesized, Yeshua is referred to as the Lamb of God six (6) times and each spelling of the word lamb is conjoined with one of the eight (8) spellings of the Name Jesus

---

[7] The Talmud – the Jewish commentary on the scriptures, states Messiah will exist 'pre-existent to the creation'

27. As prophesized, Yeshua, 'the Lamb of God' opens not His mouth cf. Is.53:7
28. As prophesized, Yeshu arose (from the dead)
29. Yeshua was 'nailed' to the cross
30. Yeshua is to 'split apart, divide, Judaism' yet never to be separate from it nor to destroy it
31. As prophesized, Yeshua is referred to as the 'Asham' – Guilt Offering i.e., the Atoning Sacrifice
32. As prophesized, Yeshua is referred to as Messiah
33. As prophesized, Yeshua is referred to as 'Anointed (One)'

Uncategorized Encryptions

34. Jesus' Hebrew Name is doubly encrypted into the text of Genesis 2:7-8 ten (10) times
35. God's Great Clue, which became our decryption key, is found in the one misspelled word in this text

Again, the question we face today is this: "Why would God take the trouble to have inserted all these encrypted revelations into the 103 letters of Genesis 2:7-8 if He did not want us to observe them and to take them to heart?" The answer is obvious; He does want us to observe them and take them to heart. Obviously, He wants each of us to experience His revelations, *today*, to reflect upon them, to be faithful to Him and to receive with great gladness His marvelous instruction.

Yet, who will accept the reality that God Himself has encrypted these revelations into the text; and, who will deny what unfolds before their eyes?" This truly is a Sinai moment for us all.

Sinai Moment

The moment I am referring to, the Sinai moment, occurred when God Himself was indisputably present upon Mt. Sinai. At that moment, all of Moses' followers were gathered at Sinai's base witnessing all *the astounding events* as Yahweh Himself dictated Torah, His teachings,[8] to the patriarch Moses. The point is this: these ancient people could not deny that it was God Who was declaring the message. They could not deny that it was God's voice which thundered off the mountain pronouncing each and every letter[9] of Torah's content nor could they deny that the Torah comprised His revealed precepts. All that they could do at that time was to hear, to understand and to decide to either follow Yahweh and obey His precepts or reject Him outright.

Just as it was in that day, so long ago, so it is today. Once again, it is Yahweh Who is calling for a response, - to accept or reject the things being revealed. The main difference is these things are being revealed not in antiquity, rather, they are being revealed to you today – in your sight and perhaps challenging your understanding. So, keep in mind, that these teachings do not originate from some person writing a book, some theologian presenting an opinion or even some religious organization promulgating a doctrine. They are from Yahweh Himself. It was He Who arranged the sequencing of the Hebrew text contained in Genesis 2:7-8 in such a way that the revelations we see today are now clearly discernable. Therefore, in a true sense, we too, today, stand at Sinai's base, marveling at these very same, Divinely pronounced, letters which to day are revealing the things unfolding before our eyes; namely the precepts and teachings of our Sovereign God. We can say this because we believe God Authored the text, the same text in which these revelations are found encrypted. The assumption which follows is that these revelations, therefore, are from Him as well. They are His direct revelations coming to light, to us, in our sight, in this day.

As I read the story of Sinai's events I am always amazed that many of Moses' followers wanted no part of

---

[8] Torah means 'teachings' – often mistranslated to mean 'Law'.
[9] The Jewish sages teach that God dictated Torah letter by painstaking letter

Yahweh's' instruction – preferring instead the idolatrous Egyptian ways so very familiar to them.

How could a people encounter the Living God and turn their backs to Him? Well, they can, they did and I'm sure some will do so today, preferring instead their 'old familiar ways' to Yahweh's unfolding revelations.

Therefore, this truly is a 'Sinai moment' for you dear reader, it is one for me as well. The options available to the people back then were only to accept Yahweh's instructions or reject them – to follow or not follow. As it turns out, if you believe God encrypted these marvelous things into His Scripture, then, these are your options as well.

Chapter 3 - First Things First – The Story Itself

The theme God brings to us in this chapter is the theme of origins:

1. origins of humanity
2. the deeper and unfathomable Mystery of Divinity i.e., – the paradoxical origin of Divinity - the Divinity about Which is said, "He is He Who is without origin"

The Surface Story

Obviously, the 'surface' story seems simple enough; and, its theme, the origins of humanity, just mentioned, is found in the 'literal read' or 'straight read' of the text. In Hebrew the straight read is called the 'pashat read'.[10]

The Pashat text relates the story of God creating man. It is about His method of forming man, enlivening man, and then establishing man in the garden located in Eden. This is a lovely story in itself. Yet, as already stated, there is much more to this story. *This is because there is another story deeply encrypted into - and* overlaid *upon the 'straight read'.*

The Hidden Story

This second story focuses upon another Being, One Who is Divine. The text itself reveals His Name, which at the time when Moses transcribed God's dictation of the Holy Torah תורה (the first five books of the Bible), this Name, obviously was known only to God. Today, this Name is

---

[10] The straight read is called 'Pashat' by the Jewish commentators. The idea behind the 'pashat read' is this: 'what you see is what you get' – the text is to be understood 'literally' when read at the pashat level. Pashat is the basic level of scriptural exegesis. No interpretation can be permitted which does not, in some context, remain relevant to the content of the pashat.

known universally i.e., the Name Yeshua – ישוע -, Jesus.[11]

Laid out, as you see the story *typically* laid out in the straight read (see below - right hand side), one would never suspect there is anything more to the text of Genesis 2:7-8 than the creation story.

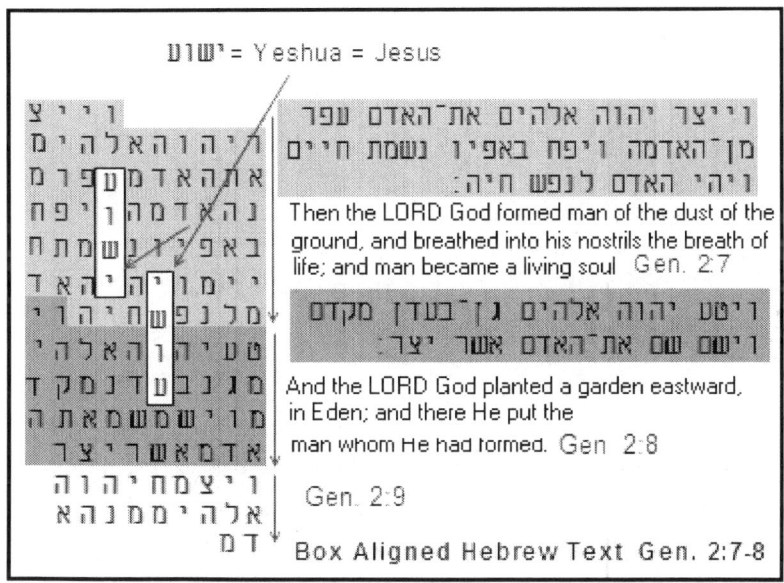

Certainly, one would never expect to see God's revelations concerning His eternal plan for Messiah and Messiahs' involvement in the salvation of human kind to be mentioned in the text of Genesis 2:7-8; yet, this is exactly what happens when one places the text into a simple 'box aligned' matrix (see above – left hand side) having, in this case, a total of 103 letters spanning across ten columns and eleven rows. The 'box aligned' text of Genesis 2:7-8 is now

---

[11] Yeshua (ישוע) is the Hebrew name we translate as Jesus – the Hebrew Name for Jesus can also be rendered as Yeshu ישו, or even Yehoshua. Although these Names were perfectly acceptable Names in first century Israel, these secondary spellings are the subject of considerable controversy today. Please read the short discussion regarding this subject in the appendix.

'visually' revealed (shaded areas) to contain a prodigious amount of here-to-fore unseen, sacred, 'Yeshuan centered' teaching, all of which teaching indisputably points to the Person of Yeshua as being exactly Who many tens of thousands of first century Jewish faithful and one and one half billions of believers today have been saying He is.

Please note: the box aligned text of Genesis 2:9 - displayed in the above illustration *is the subject of another study* and contains eight columns not ten. It is included here because there is a small, but crucial, amount of overlapping revelation between Gen. 2: 8 and Gen. 2:9 which directly connects to this study. I have not used any findings in Gen. 2:9 in the computation of the statistics and probabilities considerations which will be briefly discussed in a few moments.

So that you may have confidence regarding the revelations God is bringing to your attention today, please spend a few moments comparing the letters in the box aligned text on the left with the typical layout of the text on the right (see above). You can do this even if you can't read Hebrew. As you do this please remember, Hebrew is read from right to left. If you read Hebrew, you already know the text is intact and complete.

1. You need to be confident that all the letters in the box aligned text are, in fact, present; and, in the same sequential order as the letters found in the typical text alignment.
2. You need to be confident that the box aligned text *has not been tampered with* so as to support any particular religious agenda.

These confidences are essential since the central point of this book is that, 'God, *not man*, placed these Yeshua related encryptions into the text. This being the case, you now have to either accept God's revelations or reject God's revelations.

The Proof That God Encrypted These Texts

The proof of this claim rests in the *scientific impossibility* that the revelations you are about to witness exist in the 103 letters of text only by blind accident' i.e., just by random chance, or unintentional coincidence.

You will note only one key difference between the two text layouts (see p.16) i.e., there are no spaces between the words in the 'box aligned text'.

Although, box aligned matrixes have long been a favored encryption device used by cryptologists from the time of the beginnings of written language, the type of encryptions you will see in this book would be impossible to cryptologists in any age because they employ a considerable mixture of crypto-logical formats all of which are perfectly 'interlaced' i.e., inter-woven, into the context of the sentences comprising the readable surface layer of the text. The encrypted words and letters 'read and flow' naturally and seem to be a natural part of the surface story; so much so, that, unless the reader was aware there was a hidden message, he or she would never even think to look deeper.

Simplicity, however, is not what we are about to encounter herein. Rather, we will see complexity layered in upon complexity, revealing more and more about the 'secret precepts' our Divine Author would have us consider today.

Some may ask, 'why did Yahweh hide His teachings this way?' I can only offer my opinion regarding this question and please remember, it is only an opinion. Firstly, we can say, 'it just simply seems to be His way to enshroud things thusly'. Looking at some of the prophecies in the Biblical text, this conclusion is obvious. Little effort is required to find instances in the Biblical text where Yahweh's prophecies are stated in impossible to understand symbols; and that, unless there were a prophet interpreting them for us, we'd never know their meaning. Secondly, I also believe God wants His children to *desire to seek Him* out. He surrounds us with His evidences in the creation, all of which evidences point to a Divine Creator. These evidences seem to 'touch' something inside us that instills in us a desire to learn more about Him. They make us want to investigate the creative act and to diligently 'seek Him out' in all that we do. About this subject, the bible teaches us:

[It is] the glory of God to conceal a thing: but the honor of kings [is] to search out a matter. Ps.25:2

God does not seem to be desirous to hide things from us; rather, He enjoys hiding things for us. It would seem that He particularly enjoyed hiding the Name of Messiah – presumably for believers to enjoy its discovery. Isn't this how all of us learn best – the process of 'experience' through investigation and discovery? The best education comes by way of our striving and earnestness and effort. Therefore, I believe God wants us to look, and look, and look - for Him! Still, as just stated – this is my opinion only.

For myself, I can safely say that each time a new revelation emerged from the text being considered, it was exciting and wonderful and joyful. It made me want to see more and to learn more. I believe this is why our Father lovingly encrypted these things into the text. Hopefully, you will feel the same way about it as well.

The Ten Double Revelations Of The Name Yeshua
In the following illustration, there is no explanation as to how these, ten *'hidden in plain sight – encrypted Hebrew spellings of the Names of Jesus'* wound up being contained in the 103 letters of Genesis 2:7-8. This is to say there is no other explanation than this singular explanation. *God put them there.*

As you consider these letters layout patterns, it is important to keep in mind that each of them forms NOT an isolated pattern; but rather, each forms a *double layout pattern*. Why I consider double patterns to be important can be best understood by comparing the upper left and the upper right patterns layouts displayed in the following illustration.

Consider for a moment the question, 'What if only *one* Finding of Yeshua's Name was to be found in the upper left pattern?

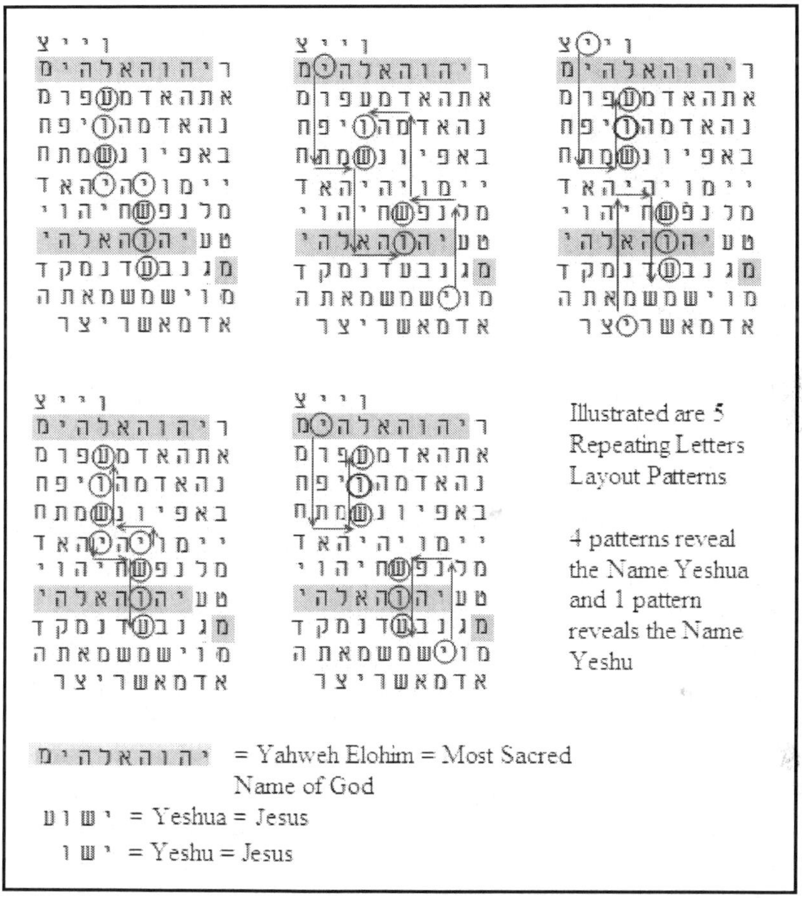

Illustrated are 5 Repeating Letters Layout Patterns

4 patterns reveal the Name Yeshua and 1 pattern reveals the Name Yeshu

מ ' ה ל א ה ו ה י = Yahweh Elohim = Most Sacred Name of God

י ש ו ע = Yeshua = Jesus

י ש ו = Yeshu = Jesus

We could still assert we are observing a pattern. The simple fact that each letter spelling His Name is neatly stacked one upon the other would certainly be hard to dismiss.

Switching over to the pattern on the upper right hand side, we now consider the same question. 'What can be said if we were to see Yeshua's Name spelled out only one time using the letters indicated in the illustration? Indeed we see three of the letters involved in spelling His Name in the text

25

stacked one upon the other, but we can't use them. The reason why this is the case is because *they, by themselves, do not spell the Name 'Yeshua'*. What is obviously missing is the letter yud - י. But which one of the many letters yud - י found in the text should we use to complete our pattern? The truth is none of the letters yud - י, when taken is isolation can be used at all; because, taken in isolation *every letter yud will 'finish the task'*. What we would wind up with is a collection of letters having 'no apparent' relationship at all. There is no 'apparent pattern' as was the case in the pattern we just finished discussing.

The first pattern we considered is called an ELS[12] columned pattern[13] and the second type, *when not taken in isolation,* is referred to as a *symmetrical letters layout pattern*.[14] We'll discuss both types of patterns later on in this book.

As we have just said, 'at first glace we're shocked to see the Name Yeshua jump off the page' just two times! Yet, herein it is seen that His Name is actually contained in the text *as a double layout pattern* ten times! Moreover there are several other places where Yeshua's Name is encrypted into the same text as a single layout pattern – we'll discuss these places later. Indeed, if one were shocked before, if one were shocked simply by observing just one double layout pattern of Yeshua's Name in this text, such a one needs now to be utterly awe-struck realizing that the Hebrew Name for Jesus is, remarkably, found encrypted into the text as a double layout pattern ten times. One should also be absolutely dumbfounded as he realizes each and every one of these ten

---

[12] See appendix i

[13] The middle pattern in the illustration is also an ELS pattern; but, obviously it is not a 'columned' pattern

[14] A symmetrical letters layout pattern, as the name suggest must posses some sort of symmetry and indeed we can observe the symmetry in our example in the repeating i.e., *doubling* of the patterns layouts. This is similar to a musical score, the symmetry is found in the repetition of the musical patterns.

findings of Jesus' Hebrew Name is deeply encrypted right into the middle of a story about which Christian believers say, He was the primary participant![15]

These revelations cannot be simply ignored. They obviously mean something and the implications of their meanings are absolutely astounding for all - be they atheists, agnostics, non-Christians or even believers in Yeshua, the Messiah.

This is because, finally, here is *proof, scientific and verifiable proof,* that a power greater than time itself has deliberately concealed within the Hebrew text of Genesis 2:7-8 the Name of Yeshua, along with an impressive, undeniable, array of critical Yeshuan teachings disputed since the time of the first century.

---

[15] Joel Young in his book Behold Yeshua, Come and See discovered the 1st pattern displayed on the left hand side of the above image. His method was a simple ELS count of ten. It was this discovery which first gained my attention. After much prayer and Gods merciful leading all the rest of the following text patterns in this book emerged and came to mind and amazingly, wherever I expected to encounter Yeshua's Name, there it was! The remainder of this book is based entirely upon Divine Revelation.

Chapter 4 - The Existence of God Proven By Science

The science about which I speak is the science of mathematics. Specifically, I am referring to the mathematical sciences of statistics and probabilities. It leaves you, as a reader, zero options to explain how these revelations happen to exist in these verses 'just accidentally'. For example, finding four letters spelling Yeshua's Name 'just one time' in this short text block, *correctly spelled*, outrageously challenges the laws of probabilities. But, finding it twice as we have found it in our first example; *and,* finding His Name being in context within the very story in which Christians agree He played the major role, pushes our statistical probabilities well past any possibility of chance happening.

Even more incredible is finding of this Name doubled ten times! Put another way, *if* Jesus' Hebrew Name had not been deliberately encrypted into the text then the odds required for these letters to be 'accidently' arranged in the text in the precise manner just spoken about, resulting in spelling Jesus' Hebrew Name a total of ten times, is reflected by the number 22^{14th} power - *against.*

What Does 22^{14th} Power Against Mean?

To illustrate what this incredible, infinitely, large number means, consider for a moment that you have 4 dice – one dice for each of the 4 Hebrew letters that spell the Name Yeshua- ישוע and each dice has 22 sides and each side of each dice carries one of the 22 letters of the Hebrew alphabet. The probabilities of just accidently spelling the Name Yeshua - just one time - *on the first throw of the dice* is 1 chance out of a possible universe of 234,256 chances (or throws of the dice) i.e., 22^{4th} power. To also spell His Name correctly on the next throw of the same four dice reduces that possibility to only one chance in 54,875,873,536 chances or -22^{8th} power. Now, consider the fact that Jesus' Name is actually contained 10 times in the 103 letters of the text. This will take us to 22^{14th} power.[16] Statistically, this pushes our probabilities well past infinity. It has just now been proven that Jesus' Name has been deliberately encrypted into the text of Genesis 2:7-8.

I used the word 'proven' because mathematicians and statisticians are universally agreed that any statistical discovery regarding any subject going beyond the number 10^{17th} power indicates a deliberateness and intention regarding the finding. Hence, in this case, we encounter deliberateness in the arrangement of the text. This can only point to a master cryptologist having the ability to weave into the 'story of the creation of Adam' the Hebrew Name of Jesus ten times!

Looking Deeper

The next two considerations in our analogy includes the ideas that Jesus' Name is found in several groupings of 'repeating patterns' and the fact that these patterns are precisely located in a story wherein He is said to be the Primary Participant.[17] These two considerations add relevancy in terms of context and purpose behind the encryptions of His Name into our text; namely, there is a Creator and His Name is Jesus. Next, there is the realization that Jesus' Name appears together with thirty five other Yeshuan i.e., Jesus centered, relevant statements concerning the Person, Nature and Mission of this One Holy Being. Thus we now see the dimension of intention layered into the story. Finally, we realize all this encrypting happened thousands of years before the fact of Jesus ever stepping foot into the creation. Therefore, we also now realize that this remarkable text conveys the indisputable flavor of 'razor sharp, accurate, foreknowledge' i.e., omniscience – a

---

[16] We are using each letter in the ten findings only one time… we are not using the same letters over and over in our calculations

[17] In the doctrines concerning Jesus, it is stated, He is the creator of all things.

Characteristic which is attached to God Alone.[18]   In a very real way, therefore, the 'existence of God' is now 'proven' by science. While this may be an odd way to express things from a believer's standpoint, this comment is made not for them; rather, it is made for the benefit of the non-believer who might be searching for such 'proof' so that he might come to faith.

Since the material which we will shortly see is now proven to be deliberately encrypted into the text, the One Who Encrypted the revelations, God, is thus proven to exist as well. After all, it takes an encryptor to encrypt a text. And remember, the encryptions of Jesus' Name into the text is just our starting point! As for what follows, there is zero possibility that the additional 30+ revelations discussed in this book are chance happenings.

The atheist and the agnostic are now confronted with 'the evidence' they have been demanding when they say, 'show us scientific proof that God exists'. They can no longer say, 'there is no proof'.

Of course the Christian believer is also impacted by these proofs. Perhaps his or her faith needed strengthening, or perhaps a call to repentance over sin might be in order. And, if they are looking for a method to evangelize those who require evidence that can be substantiated by science, they now have what they need.

Regarding any well-intentioned people who worship outside the Jewish or Christian faiths, here is a call to heed God's invitation to consider what is laid out before your eyes. The God of the Christians and the Jews is also revealing Himself to you today in a manner which transcends any possibility of refutation.

The question remains open, however, as to how Jewish readers, who have not accepted Yeshua as their Messiah,

---

[18] The preexistence of the content of Genesis 2:7-8 relative to the time of Yeshua as proven by recent archeological finds is important because it eliminates any possibility that these texts were inserted 'after the first century' to support Christian teaching.

might view these revelations - especially in considering the fact that Jewish teaching opines as to how the five Books of Moses came into being in the first place. They have been taught the entire Torah – תורה – (the first five books of Moses) was dictated to Moses by God – letter by painstaking letter.   Therefore, they believe the Torah is absolutely authoritative since it was originally dictated by God.

Ironically, they are now confronted with the reality that the very thing they considered authoritative and so greatly beloved is presenting teachings about the Person of Jesus, which teachings, are not generally well accepted in the Jewish camp i.e., Jesus is Messiah and He is God.

Concerning Torah Accuracy

The flawless transmission of the Torah throughout the millennia has been the singular and greatest endeavor of the Jewish sages. Says the Midrash[19] (Devarim Rabba 9:4)[20]

> "Before his death, Moses wrote 13 Torah Scrolls. Twelve of these were distributed to each of the 12 Tribes. The 13th was placed in the Ark of the Covenant (with the Tablets). If anyone would come and attempt to rewrite or falsify the Torah, the one in the Ark would "testify" against him. (Likewise, if he had access to the scroll in the Ark and tried to falsify it, the distributed copies would "testify" against him.)"[21]

---

[19] The Midrash is a homiletic method of Biblical exegesis. A Midrash can begin with a verse or even a word and usually expands into a loosely contextual teaching which seeks to derive the meaning of the text.
[20] commentary on the Book of Deuteronomy
[21] http://www.simpletoremember.com/articles/a/torahaccuracy/

Also illustrating the great concern the Jewish people have regarding Torah accuracy is another famous story in the Talmud[22] (Eruvin 13a)

> When Rabbi Meir came to Rabbi Yishmael to learn Torah, he was asked: "What is your profession, my son?" "I am a scribe," was the reply. He said to me: "My son, be careful with your work, for it is the work of Heaven. Should you perhaps omit one letter or add one letter—it could result that you destroy the entire world[23]

> Maharsha,[24] explains there is a danger even if the error does not affect the meaning of the word. This is because of a tradition that the letters of the Torah form the sacred Names of God written as "black fire upon white fire." These letters were employed by God in creating the world, and it is through them that He sustains it. The deletion of even one letter of this 'sustaining force' therefore threatens the existence of the world. Hence, the letter perfect transmission of the Torah has been a Jewish priority throughout the centuries.[25]

Because of these 'traditions', the Jews have an incredible respect for every 'letter', every 'jot' and every 'tittle' in the text. This reverence for each letter in the scripture forms the underpinning for their almost flawless transmission of the scriptural text over these last several millennia. A few more quotations are illustrative of this point.

---

[22] Talmud is a collection of scriptural commentary offered by the chief teachers of Judaism and provides a plethora of opinions regarding scriptural content.

[23] Ibid.

[24] 16th century Poland

[25] Ibid.

" Should you omit or add even one single letter to or from the Torah, you would thereby destroy all the universe." (unknown)

"There is not a single letter in the Torah on which but a thousand secrets hang." Menashe Ben Israel

Every letter has a soul." Moses Cordovero

"Every letter is a whole universe." The Maggid of Mezhirich

Thousands of other such opinions can be easily offered as well. The point is this; all of us today owe our profound gratitude to the Jewish people for their unexcelled diligence in the protection of God's Most Holy Scripture.

Ironically, the deep reverence of the Jews 'for the text' now creates a challenging crisis in faith for them i.e., the resultant dilemma of finding Yeshua's Name in the 'Creation Story' text co-embedded within scores of other key 'Yeshuan revelations'. Therefore, the obvious question they, and all readers, should now be asking is repeated here:

"Why would God dictate His text – 'letter by letter' to His servant Moses in such a way that with nothing more than a simple 'box alignment' of the letters, the Person of Yeshua is revealed and several core Christian teachings are now also shockingly evidenced in the very act of the creation of mankind"?

So, there is a riddle to be solved here. However, it's really not such a tough riddle to solve, is it? The answer is obvious. The real problem is this: if you are Jewish and do not believe Yeshua is the Messiah, you are now being challenged by the very Author of Genesis 2:7-8 to rethink your opinion. You will have to decide if what is laid out before your eyes is deliberately embedded in the text by God. If you decide yes, you must take action.

a. You may have to make decisions which may put you at odds with family and friends.
b. You will have to believe Yeshua is dearly loved by 'the Father'.
c. You will have to personally, accept Him as your Messiah and believe He is the Father's 'Only Begotten Son'.

However, Your decision does not even remotely suggest you have to stop being Jewish.

The core issue is only this:

Messiah has come!
So, rejoice! Go meet Him!

How do you do this? Just keep Him in Mind as you live your daily life (see the chapter, 'What Do I Do Now' for more information). Keep Him in mind as you celebrate your feasts. Learn, 'as best you can', how His presence is interwoven through the teachings regarding the festivals. Read the 'Torah of Messiah' (the New Testament). Live your life accordingly. You may want to share this book with a friend and help him or her to rejoice in Messiah. You may want to attend a Messianic Synagogue. The point to all this is simple. You don't have to stop being Jewish in order to rejoice in your Messiah. So, why not stay Jewish?

You see, Yeshua was a Jew, His disciples were Jews, and His teachings were given to the 'Jews first then to the gentiles'.[26] He preached in the synagogues of the Jews and kept the festivals of the Jews. Moreover, He taught nothing

---

[26] Cf., Rom. 1:16, 2:9, 2:10

which was not to be found in the scripture and the tradition of the Jews and His life and ministry brought to fruition all the many wonderful things that the Jewish people for such a long time longed and hoped for.[27] He did not destroy Torah[28] as those antagonistic to Judaism claim; rather, He fulfilled Torah.

He, Himself, has become the Living Torah. He said,

> Think not that I am come to destroy the law (Torah) or the prophets: I am not come to destroy, but to fulfill them (i.e., to overflowing) Matt. 5:7

The following is the Greek rendering of the same passage.

> Μὴ νομίσητε ὅτι ἦλθον καταλῦσαι τὸν νόμον[29], ἢ τοὺς προφήτας οὐκ ἦλθον καταλῦσαι, ἀλλὰ πληρῶσαι[30]

Notice the footnote for the word νόμον. This word points to the established 'customs of the Jews'. Yeshua is saying very emphatically that He did not come to destroy the customs of the Jews. Rather, He came to fulfill them to the full, to make them to abound – this is the meaning of the Greek word πληρῶσαι i.e., to make (the thing) abound – to allow a thing its full expression. One of Yeshua's Messianic goals resulting from His incarnation into the creation was to attach onto the Law of the Jews ..., 'Himself' –Who Is - the fullest expression of their Law i.e., teaching, i.e., Torah!

---

[27] We will have more to say on this subject in a later chapter.
[28] Incorrectly translated into Greek then English as 'law' rather than 'teachings'/
[29] νόμος anything established, anything received by usage, custom, or tradition
[30] to make full, to fill up, i.e. to fill to the full; to cause to abound.
Strong's unabridged concordance of the Old and New Testament

To cast the law, the teaching, the Torah aside is tantamount to casting Yeshua aside. Jesus Himself said the law bears witness to Him.

Indeed, the many beautiful festivals kept by your people actually point to the person of Yeshua. But this fact is a subject for another book. The simple point is this, accepting Yeshua to be Who God is herein revealing Him to be does not require you to reject Judaism, your family or your customs rather it completes your Judaism i.e., Messiah has come. No longer are you a Jew who waits, ..., *the wait is now over*!

Yet, *your decision has a spiritual dimension of eternal significance*. Along with your 'decision to accept and embrace' the Father's begotten Son, Yeshua, comes the gifts of the redemption from the effects of sin and everlasting salvation – a salvation freely granted by the Father to all who trust in the promises of the scripture through belief in His Son, the Messiah of Israel.

Beyond the Probabilities

The next several revelations will continue to take you beyond any possibility of *mere coincidence* being at work in what God is laying out before your eyes. You are now invited to behold the Revelations of the Most High God – revealed in His Torah – letter by letter. The revelations you are about to see have both a quantitative and a theological value.

The Quantitative Value in Finding Yeshua's Name

Even though the fact that Jesus' Name being encrypted into the account of the creation of humanity might be challenging to some readers, one cannot simply expunge Yeshua's name from the story for the sake of opinion, or deeply seated religious belief, or even simple preference. Obvious? Perhaps it is obvious, yet, this is an important point. Some would rather not see this Name in the text at all! Consider the fact that, to remove all ten occurrences of

His Name would remove a considerable portion of the Pashat text i.e., the straight read of Genesis 2:7-8! Consider the damage this would do to God's Authoritative Word.

Consider as well the fact that the sheer *quantity* of the occurrences of the Hebrew spellings of Jesus Name obviates all possibility of random chance being a being a possible explanation as to how His Name found its way into the text. The conclusion we have reached regarding this remarkable fact is, God Himself wants Jesus' Name to be in the text of Genesis 2:7-8! Therefore, to expunge this Name from the text is to defy Yahweh Himself!

Theological Value in Finding Yeshua's Name

Jewish exegetes teach that each and every letter contained in these verses is sacred and therefore it possesses 'theological value'. Perhaps, the true theological value regarding these encryptions is this fact; *God is announcing His Hidden Secret* that Yeshua is the Creator, Yeshua is His begotten Son and Yeshua is the Messiah of Israel. One cannot simply alter the Torah for reasons of political correctness or religious preference – one *must* consider the information which it presents even if this information is inconvenient or troublesome. This obligation includes the astounding truth that Jesus' Name and thirty-five teachings regarding His Messiahship have an unmistakable, undeniable, presence in the scriptural text which describes the creation.

Chapter 5 - Yahweh and Yeshua A Paradoxical Unity

If one were to remove all evidence of Jesus' Hebrew Name from the text contained in Genesis 2:7-8 he would have also done damage to both occurrences of the most Holy Name of God, Yahweh Elohim יהוהאלהימ , (the Name which is above all Names). For example, in the following illustration, if Jesus' Name were to be expunged from the text the spelling of Yahweh Elohim would be damaged as well. This is because two of these spellings of Jesus' name are inextricably connected to the Divine Name, the Tetragrammaton[31].

According to the Jewish sages, if one were bold enough to delete Jesus' Name form the text, thus-by severely damaging the text, he would have destroyed the universe many times over. The reason they give is, 'it is His Name (God's Name) which holds all things together'! We concur with this teaching.

The conclusion is, Yahweh and Yeshu, Jesus cannot be separated, they are One. Yahweh deliberately set into

---

[31] Tetragrammaton (from the Greek τετραγράμματονw, meaning '[word of] four letters' (tetra "four" + gramma (gen. grammatos) "letter"), refers to יהוה, Yahweh, a name used by the Hebrew Masoretic Text to refer to the deity of the Israelites. The Jewish conception of God holds that this is one of several names for the deity. Wiki. Tetragrammaton, July 7, 2009.

place the inextricable sharing of letters which reveals this fact. So let's pause for a moment to discuss what is meant by the term 'inextricable connection'.

About Inextricable Connections

In the above illustration we see two examples of inextricable connections. Looking at the topmost 'inextricable connection' we see the sharing of the Hebrew letter yud – י - in both the Names Yeshu and Yahweh Elohim. Following the spelling of Yeshu's Name downward we see it terminating in the bottommost spelling of the Name Yahweh Elohim at the letter vav – ו. [32] This type of connection is seen by the Jewish sages to reflect an 'ontological unity'.[33] Should one remove either Hebrew letter from either spelling of these Names then both Names fall apart. For this reason we state that such letter sharing produces an inextricable connection i.e., one cannot extract

---

[32] According to Jewish tradition the letter vav means 'nail' or 'join' Yeshua is joined to YHVH in an 'inextricable unity of essence' also Yeshu was nailed to the cross in His execution. Both meanings apply.
[33] Ontology (from the Greek ὄν, genitive ὄντος: "of that which is", and -λογία, -logia: science, study, theory) is the philosophical study of the nature of being, existence or reality as such, as well as the basic categories of being and their relations. Wiki. Ontology. In short, ontology is the study of 'beingness'.

the inextricable 'item' – whatever that item might be - without damaging or destroying the item itself. In this case the items we are discussing are two very important Names.

That this inextricable connectivity even exists, the Jewish exegetes would say, 'has to mean something'. They would also have to agree, that the fact that the Name Yeshua – pictorially - proceeds out from the Name of the Eternal One, Yahweh Elohim, blessed be He, *and that Yeshua's Name also – pictorially - recedes* back into Yahweh Elohim – just as the Christians profess-, '*this too has to mean something as well';* and, it does. It means something very obvious.

The *rabbinic conclusion* would agree, 'because Yahweh so carefully arranged the letters of both *Their* Names so that they cannot be separated then*, "in some sense, Both are One;* yet, when one considers the box aligned text from a pictorial standpoint, both Names still are separate i.e., unique.[34] A true paradox i.e., a unity that bespeaks of separateness.

Looking deeper still, Jewish tradition teaches concerning both inextricable letters. The letter yud י by itself means God and the letter vav – ו - has as its meaning – an act of joining together, *'pinning or nailing' (understood this way, the two meanings of the letters can be understood to mean 'God nailed' i.e., crucified!)* Our revelation is now being pushed in two directions at the same time.

---

[34] The 1st council in Nicea c. 325, included in the draft of the creed the following language "[But those who say: 'There was a time when he was not;' and 'He was not before he was made;' and 'He was made out of nothing,' or 'He is of another substance' or 'essence,' or 'The Son of God is created,' or 'changeable,' or 'alterable'—they are condemned by the holy catholic and apostolic Church.]" Whenever I am referring to this Mystery I use the phrase a 'multiplicity of Persona within a singularity of Godhead'.

1. It reveals the eternal Mystery of the Holy Unity i.e.,
   Yeshua is in some sense One within Deity – eternally
   con-joined within it
2. It suggests, the Yeshuan self-less act of atonement
   sacrifice

Herein is the Mystery of the ages being revealed in your
sight. Both *Yahweh and Yeshua are One - yet both are
unique.* The Holy One, first draws us in with His broad, easy
to see inextricably connected Hebrew letters then once we
see this, the teaching gets deeper and deeper. Isn't this a
remarkable way to encounter God's revelation?

Supporting the conclusion just made, above, here is
another revelation which emphasizes the point. It clearly
teaches Yeshua is (Adonai) God revealed!

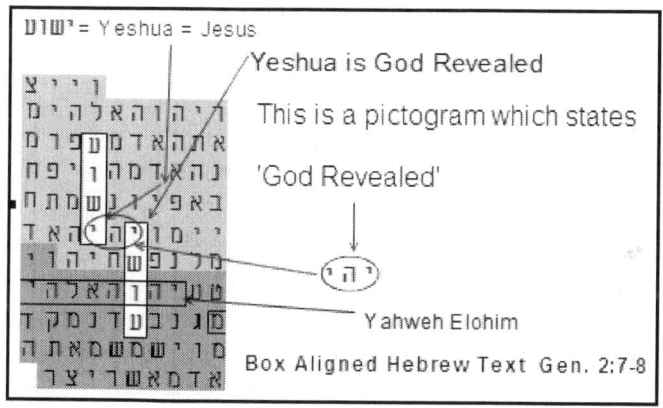

God is intent upon teaching Yeshua is God Revealed.
This He does by embedding into the text a special linguistic
device called a pictogram, which, because it is inextricably
joined to both of the Names Yeshua, imbues each of the
Names Yeshua with the meaning which the pictogram
conveys i.e., Yeshua is revealed to be, 'God Revealed'!
Also, notice the manner in which the text is laid out i.e., the
Name Yeshua does not intersect with Yahweh's Name when
the Name Yeshua is shown ascending in its spelling; but,

Yeshua's Name *does* intersect with Yahweh's Name when it is shown descending in its spelling. Accordingly, the intimation is clear: although in some sense Yeshua and Yahweh Elohim are One, inextricably One, hence consubstantial, the unfathomable nature of this unity seems to differ based upon the location Each occupies.

More About Pictograms

Ancient Hebrew writing is similar to Chinese and ancient Egyptian writing in that every word was formed by adding "pictures" together to "paint" or illustrate 'the meaning' the author wishes to convey. In ancient Hebrew each 'written character' conveys a 'pictorial meaning'. The combination of these meanings is the message proffered by the pictogram.

In the above 'pictogram[35] we see God has joined the two encryptions spelling Yeshua's Name by a subtle and easily missed revelation which is circled. The interpretation of this pictogram is *Yeshua is God revealed.* We arrive at this meaning as follows: the double pictographic *parent* image of - יי - is understood to mean Adonai, 'the Lord', i.e., 'God'. When the pictographic Symbol – ה - is paced between *parent* images like it is in the notation יהי, it suggests the 'idea of revealing' the meaning conveyed by the *parent* image. The parent image, of course, is – יי - which means Adonai, God. Therefore, what we see stated 'pictographically' is *God Revealed*; and, because this notation is inextricably connected to the 'written out' Name Yeshua, we conclude it is Yeshu Who is being referenced as 'God revealed'.

---

[35] A pictograph also called pictogram or pictogramme is an ideogram that conveys its meaning through its pictorial resemblance to a physical object. Earliest examples of pictographs include ancient or prehistoric drawings or paintings found on rock walls. Pictographs are also used in several writing and graphic systems. It is a basis of Hebrew, Chinese languages also cuneiform and, to some extent, hieroglyphic writing, which uses drawings also as phonetic letters or determinative rhymes.

The Level Of 'Drash'

There is still more which can be concluded if we observe these revelations from a deeper exegetical perspective, the 'Jewish exegetical level' of Drash, i.e., the level of allegory and typology.[36] As mentioned a moment ago, what we see revealed in the box-aligned text which was just discussed is an ascendant and a descendant *relationship* – a *relationship within Deity* which differs upon location – the locals being Heaven and earth. It is an eternal and a temporal relationship, a dual relationship. Please keep this word in mind, 'dual'.

In the heavenly abode prior to the creation, He Whom we call Yeshua had a different type of relationship with the Father than He enjoyed when He walked upon the earth.

In the pre-creation epoch, the relationship was obviously purely spiritual. It had the characteristics of a perfect unity within Divinity which is perfectly manifested in Its individuated separateness. Our God is a God of Paradox. He is One in Multiplicity. He is One and yet is not Alone.

In the earthly mode, the relationship was also dual i.e., Yeshua was the God-Man, fully God and fully man. The mirrored image revealed in the illustration can certainly be suggesting that He Who had exclusively dwelt in the 'spiritual abode' lowered Himself to become man, uniting Himself with mankind's flesh within the abode of temporality, yet remaining inextricably connected to and One within Yahweh Elohim. Moreover, the human flesh He betook upon Himself is known to many by the Name 'Yeshua', Jesus. We are taught, He became one like us,

---

[36] Typology is a theory of exegesis which admits to seeing the whole story of the Jewish and Christian peoples as shaped by God, with past events and persons within the story acting as symbols and types for later events.

taking upon Himself our human nature 'created in the image of God' [37]

All of this is to say that we see *evidenced* in the ascending spelling of Yeshua's Name the things which speak to the eternal relationship Yeshua has with the Eternal One. We see in the descending spelling of Yeshua's Name the things which speak of the earthly walk of Yeshua and His dual Nature, i.e., His Divine and His human natures; and implicitly, His mission upon the earth.

May He ever be Blessed! Our God is today allowing all of us at this moment, to witness that which 'eye has never seen' – 'to hear that which ear has never heard!'[38]

Letter Sharing

It would seem natural for some to object saying, 'exegetical comments' based on such things as letter sharing, or even letters removal, seems a bit contrived'; but, as any 'old testament' exegete will tell you, this method, as I have employed it, perfectly agrees with acceptable rabbinic practice. For example, in the Midrash Rabbah[39] on Genesis, concerning God's renaming of Abram, is included this noteworthy comment from the renowned Jewish exegete R. Nehemiah,

"The Holy One, blessed be He, united His Name with Abraham".

Note, the sages' reference in this example concerns God uniting His name to Abram's. *This, God does via the process of letter sharing.* As just mentioned, the reference speaks about the changing of the Name from Abram to Abraham when Abram accepts circumcision as a *sign of the covenant* established between himself and God. The Holy

---

[37] The spiritual became carnal that the carnal might become spiritual. This is what the ancient theologians referred to as Theosis

[38] Is. 64:4

[39] a rabba is a commentary in the form of parables

One inserts the letter 'hey – ה' into Abrams name. Abram now becomes, *the one* who now is, in some sense, transformed *in his person* 'to be' a bearer or revealer of grace and blessing. He is *revealed* to be *the one* who manifests Gods abiding presence: He is now Abraham.

In this regard, Abraham's name now does double duty. Remove the 'hey' and the patriarch goes back to being a simple leader of his clan. Insert the 'hey – ה' and Abraham's name identifies both, the person of the patriarch, just as any name identifies it's bearer, and also reveals Abraham as the 'one' who is in his 'being' the *revealer*[40] of the indwelling God and 'the blessing of the Most High'.

Supporting this view, we must also consider that a great portion of Jewish mysticism, Kabbalah[41] and Zohar[42] involves letters substitutions, letters swapping and letters re-arranging. While the reader may not consider the writings just cited as worthy of reading and studying, *these documents, however, do point to the fact that letters sharing and letters substitution or swapping occupy an acceptable position in theological practice in so far as Jewish sensibilities are concerned.*

In summary, what God has revealed herein is the teaching that the incarnated Yeshua and The Lord God, Yahweh Elohim are in some paradoxical fashion unique yet, One and undivided. There exists an 'Inextricable Unity'

---

[40] See the discussion on the sub topic 'God Revealed' and the Hebrew letter Hey - ה

[41] Kabbalah (Hebrew: קַבָּלָה, lit. "receiving") is an ancient discipline and school of thought concerned with the mystical aspects of Judaism it should not be confused with the 'diabolical pop culture trend' we see popularized today.

[42] The Zohar (Hebrew: זֹהַר, lit. *Splendor* or *Radiance*) is widely considered the most important work of Kabbalah, or Jewish mysticism. It is a mystical commentary on the Torah (the five books of Moses), written in medieval Aramaic. It contains a mystical discussion of the nature of God, the origin and structure of the universe, the nature of souls, sin, redemption, good and evil, and the relationship between en God and man. Wikki. Zohar. 06/04/09.

which applies to these two Names. In a real sense, according to the Jewish sages, the connection between such 'enmeshed words' is seen as an 'ontological unity', i.e., a unity in terms of 'beingness hence, *essence*'. Both are, 'one in essence and undivided'[43] i.e., cannot be divided. Obviously prior to the creation, as mentioned before, the Name Yeshu was known, eternally, only to God. Only God knew Who and What Yeshua is i.e., His Only Begotten Son Who will be incarnated upon the earth and be known to all men by the Name Yeshua; and, Who will be known to some men by the titles, 'God revealed' and Messiah.

God Is Still Revealed *Even Without A Pictogram*

By now the reader ought not be surprised to hear it said that we can still look deeper into this revelation. By so doing we again see the incredible teaching regarding the unity between Yeshu i.e., Jesus and Yahweh.

---

43 The Nicene Creed

In a most marvelous way, God has arranged this particular text so that the pictographic meanings just discussed, may be seen revealed in the actual words contained in the text. To do this we simply *read words* rather than *observing a pictograph*. We now see a dual 'mirrored letters pattern' emerge which twice spells the Name 'Yah'– הי, i.e., Yahweh. One Name 'Yahweh' is read right to left – in a forward fashion -, One Name "Yahweh' is read left to right – in a reversed fashion.[44]! Regardless of the the reading direction, the Name 'Yah' is clearly inextricable from each of the two Names Yeshua thus supporting the idea of a Holy Consubstantial Unity.

Yeshua Is The Very Condition Of Existence Itself
We'll still look a little deeper.

1. Yeshua Is The Word Of God
2. Yeshua is the 'Creating Word' of God, the 'Self Existent One'

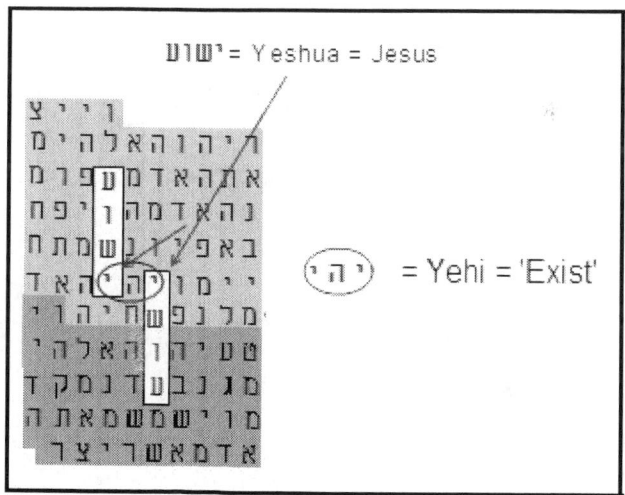

_____

[44] 'Yah' is not an abbreviation of the Name Yahweh it is an accepted Name of God which means exactly what the Name Yahweh means.

Let's turn to the three letters themselves - yehi – יהי pronounced, ya-hee. Although יהי is not generally employed as an actual *word* in the scripture we do observe one notable exception. It is used as a Holy Command in Genesis 1. *It is the actual creative command pronounced by God Himself.*

The command proceeds outwardly, from deep within Godhead,[45] and by it all things were made. In all, yehi – יהי – is proclaimed 20 times in Genesis 1. God proclaims, 'Exist!' – יהי – and, 'it becomes to exist'. Furthermore, Jewish theology teaches yehi – יהי – *is also the actual condition existence itself.*

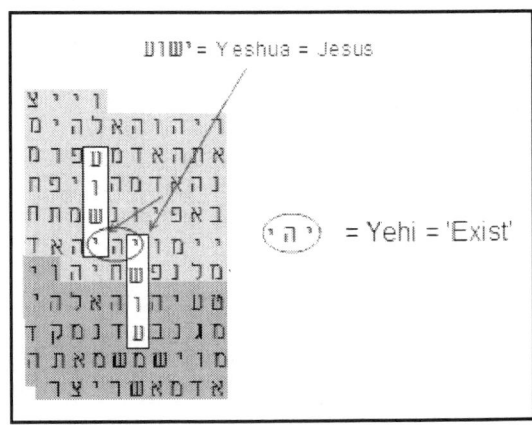

Borrowing a term from Martin Buber[46], it can be said yehi – יהי – is the 'I-ness of God'. It is not only the Divine Proclamation 'Exist!', yehi – יהי – is the Holy 'condition' of existing in the purest ontological sense. It is God being revealed in the fullness of His Pre-incarnate Divinity i.e., as a verb, *'Existing'* or the *'Existing One'*. Yehi is the Divine action manifest as the *'Word of God'*, thus, Yehi is God revealed as the condition of 'self-existence' – the Holy 'I',

---

[45] Nicene Creed

[46] I and Thou, Martin Buber ,is the theological doctrine of the direct, mutual relation between beings. Within the Mystery of Divinity, it is a relation in terms of ontology.

without Which, utter chaos is the everlasting state of affairs. In this sense yehi can also be understood as a noun. יהי enters chaos (that which is non-existing) and existence 'becomes into being.

Still looking deeper. In support of this teaching we find another revelation hidden in this same spot. It is the word אהיה – Ehyeh – 'I Am or I Will Be.

> I Am that I Am אֶהְיֶה אֲשֶׁר אֶהְיֶה, pronounced *Ehyeh asher ehyeh* is a common English translation of the response God used in the Hebrew Bible when Moses asked for His name (Exodus 3:14). It is one of the most famous verses in the Torah. Ehyeh is the first person singular imperfect form and is usually translated in English Bibles as "I will be" (or "I shall be"), for example, at Exodus 3:12. *Ehyeh asher ehyeh* is generally interpreted to mean *I am that I am*, though it can also be translated as "I-shall-be that I-shall-be." (often contracted in English as *"I AM"*) is one of the Seven Names of God.   Wikipedia.org

The phrase, I Am, (Hayah) - see below - encrypted *in reverse spelling*, links both Names 'Yeshua' and the phrase, I Am thus indicating it is Yeshua Who is inextricably One with God's Self Declared Name, 'IAm'.

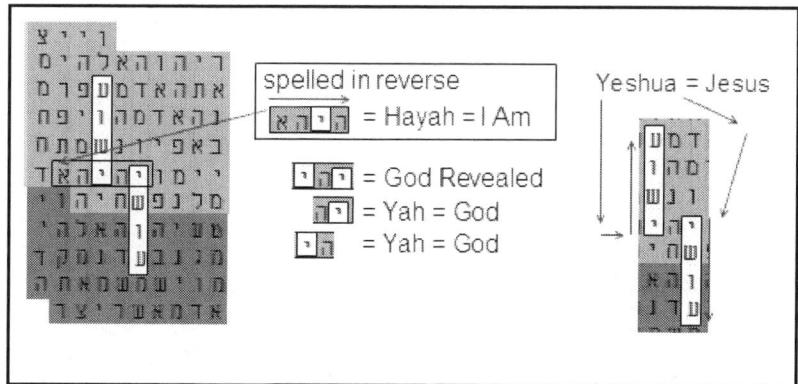

It would seem that His eternal relationship with the Father, as we have already discussed, is in the capacity of Being[47] 'the Word', in contrast however, we can now also see the relationship He had with Moses in the realm of the creation was as the 'I Am'.

It becomes astounding that the Holy Name 'I Am' is also inextricable from the pictogram which says 'God Revealed' and both Names are attached to *Both revelations of the Name Yeshua.* The fact that Deity was revealing Himself to the patriarch when He revealed to Moses His Name adds tremendous context to the revelations found in Genesis 2:7-8 since the Creator is also understood by both Jews and Gentiles to be the Divinity Who proclaims Himself to be the "I Am'.

Therefore, here deeply encrypted into a text about the creation is God Himself revealing Himself to be the Creator the 'I Am, Whom mankind will later come to know as Yeshua! And now, He is revealing Himself to you!

Truly, it is humbling to witness God' astounding, razor sharp, clear revelation made via these three, easy to overlook, letters.

Yahweh has spoken; Yeshua is the 'Creating Word' of God, the 'Self Existent One'.[48] In the second mirrored image pattern (page 19), the direction of the spelling of Yeshu's Name is reversed. The spelling on the right ascends and the spelling on the left descends. In the first pattern discussed, the spelling on the right descended and on the left ascended.

---

[47] I've used capitals here because I am referring to God. It is very awkward to speak of God this way. He is a verb, yet the only way to refer to Him in the eternal realm is as a Being i.e., a Divine Noun

[48] 'ever existing and eternally the same', Nicene Creed.

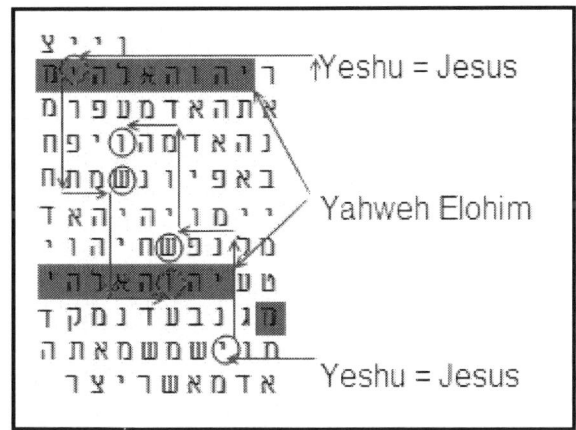

This has to mean something – well at least that's what a rabbi would say. To discern one of the possible meanings which this bi-directional spelling revelation could suggest let's compare the pictorial presentations of two Names - Yeshu, Jesus. You'll notice in the above boxed aligned text, the leftmost spelling of the Name Yeshu proceeds forth from the ineffable Name Yahweh Elohim יהוה אלהים and terminates into a separate spelling of the Name Yahweh Elohim יהוה אלהים. Keeping in mind what has been previously said, 'that the scripture covered in the lower portions of the box aligned text seems to refer to earthly matters', what we can therefore conclude is being revealed in this illustration is focused upon the descent of Divinity into the creation. This Divine Being, Who is descending into the creation, is revealed to be inextricably One within Yahweh Elohim in both spellings of this most exalted Name, יהוה אלהים. And, once again, this Being is revealed to be none other than Yeshu, Jesus – see the box aligned text.

Additionally, we note the 'descending' spelling of Yeshu's Name, terminates at the letter vav ו, found in the second spelling of the Name Yahweh Elohim. As we just discussed, the meaning of the letter vav is, 'to nail'. In analyzing this revelation we can certainly add this amazing revelation to the ones we already have and say God became

the man Jesus in order to be nailed to the cross while yet remaining both God and Man. This is what the first century Jewish, Messianic, believers in Yeshua taught; and, this remains the teaching of the church they birthed, even unto this very day. The implication is both stunning and elegant i.e., in some sense both are One yet distinct. Yeshu and Yahweh are in some unfathomable and sublime way One. Yeshu is One within Yahweh Elohim and differentiated apart from Yahweh Elohim. Yeshu is 'the paradoxical latent presence of change within the changeless'.[49] So, now our basic question becomes more
pointed:

> *"Why would God dictate His text – 'letter by letter' in such a way that with nothing more than a simple 'box alignment' of the letters, the Person of Yeshua is* clearly *revealed and several core Christian teachings are now shockingly evidenced in the very story of the creation of mankind - a story in which it is said Yeshua is the primary participant"?*

Why indeed? There is an obvious hermeneutical[50] inference which can be made at this juncture, namely, *God wants all people, especially His 'chosen people', to know about the Being we refer to as Yeshua; and, He wants all of us to deepen our commitment to His beloved Son, the Begotten One , begotten of the Father before all ages.*

Let's take a moment to go over a few of the things God would have us know about Yeshua and the clue which he encrypted into the text which serves to bring these things to our attention.

---

[49] We'll speak more on this subject in a moment
[50] Biblical hermeneutics is the study of the principles of interpretation concerning the books of the Bible. Wiki., hermanuetic.

Chapter 6 - The Clue

God's primary clue, pointing to the fact that there is something more to the story, is found in the first word in the text of the story related by Genesis 2:7, וייצר, vayyitser – (and He formed).

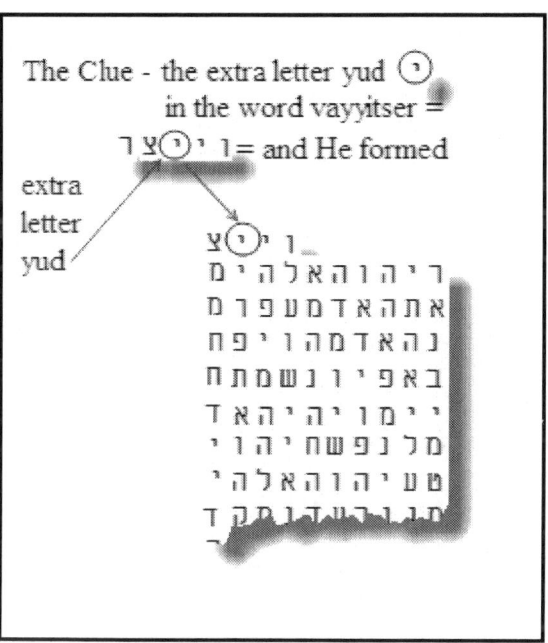

The word *vayyitser is misspelled* in that it contains two letters yud י. Rabbinic scholars, being 'rabbinic scholars', could not possibly allow this 'error' to go unchallenged. They reasoned, 'Such spelling anomalies must mean something'. 'Surely, God can spell, yet, this word is misspelled'! 'God must be making a point'. These same sages have historically offered several theories to the faithful to consider. For example, one rabbi speculates that God's point regarding the 'double yud' is to denote the seventh and ninth month of pregnancy.[51] Another rabbi

---

[51] J. Yebamoth 4:2, T.S. 2, 113.

offers the speculation the double yud denotes the two inclinations in man (one toward good the other toward evil).[52]

We nevertheless find in the Tractate Berakoth of the Babylonian Talmud 61a., T.S. 2, 113, a completely different idea, the statement,

> "(this)….. scripture writes 'vayyitser' with the letter yud repeated to signify a double creation".

Obviously, the idea of a *double anything* is particularly appealing for us to consider especially in light of the mirrored i.e., doubled, mirror-image patterns just discussed which reference Yeshua's Name.

A Double Creation

What can this mean, a 'double creation'? The answer to this question is astonishing and has a great deal to do with the Hebrew word we translate as 'Genesis' i.e., 'Bereshit'[53] - בְּרֵאשִׁית which is often translated by the word, 'creation'.

The 'literal' meaning of Bereshit'- בְּרֵאשִׁית is 'origin'. Please keep this in mind. Also keep in mind that the subject 'on the table', in the Pashat read, the literal read, is the creation or 'origin' of the first things, in particular, mankind. By way of contrast, however, it is also clear by now while the straight read of the story is about the creation of humankind, the revelations we have been dealing with are not exclusively about the origin of man; but, also about the Origin and Person and Ministry of Yeshua. 'He who is of God and is God, He Who is Begotten and not made, He Who

---

[52] R. Nahman b. R. Hisda.
[53] **Genesis** (Greek: Γένεσις, meaning "birth", "creation", "cause", "beginning", "source" or "origin") Genesis is the first book of the Torah, the Tanakh, and the Old Testament of the Bible. Its Hebrew spelling is בְּרֵאשִׁית, B'reshit or Bərêšîth, meaning *"in the beginning"*. It is the first word in the Bible.

is of One substance with the Father and by Whom all things were made'[54]

Until now, Christians have been trusting in this 'teaching' *by faith* – essentially faith alone. Now, herein God is doing something different – He is providing verifiable proof concerning the teachings regarding Yeshua. Certainly it is difficult for many to accept on faith 'what eye has not seen'. So, God has wondrously placed into the box aligned text, 'that which eye *can* see' i.e., the Revelation of God's Holy Mystery for us to ponder in awestruck humility.

Back to the Rabbis

The Rabbinic ideas we have just mentioned attempt to serve the purpose of explaining God's apparent spelling error. Caution warns us however, these rabbinic ideas still remain to be nothing more than mere speculations, opinions, or pious commentaries. They offer 'no evidence' that their proffered explanations are true.

Begotten Son Of The Father

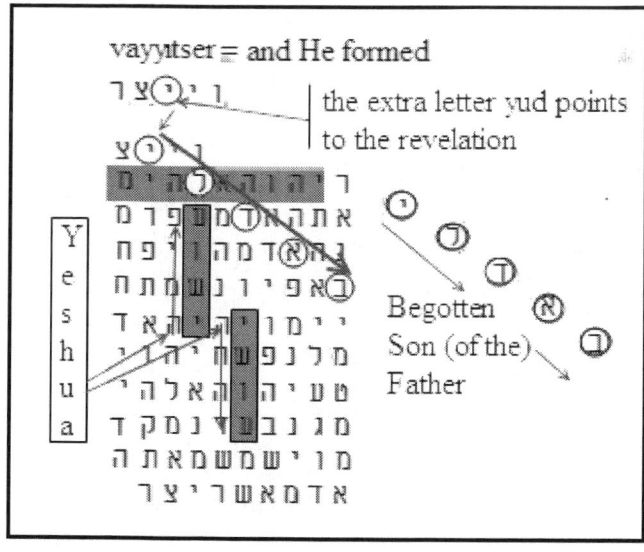

---

[54] Nicene Creed

The extra letter yud found in the misspelled word vayyitser וַיִּיצֶר which means, 'and He formed' becomes the first letter in the phrase 'yeleed ab – יְלֶדאַב' which means boy of the father'. In the box aligned text we see this term running diagonally through and inextricably connected to the sacred Name Yahweh Elohim. Hence, in some sense, the Begotten of the Father is One with and within Yahweh Elohim.

While this revelation is a most wondrous thing we need to pause for a moment and consider what might be going on which may not be not so wonderful for some believers. It would seem at this point that our theology is being directed by God Himself. Therefore, in a true sense, each of us are being 'weighed and measured'[55] by God Himself. God is now holding us accountable for what He is revealing to us. God is asking, "Will you *now believe* the writing on the wall, the evidence I am placing before your eyes?" "Will you now believe Yeshua is my Only begotten Son and that salvation comes by way of Him alone?'

I am reminded of what the word says, 'if you have been given much, much will be expected of you.' We now clearly understand the reason for the so-called 'Divine Spelling Mistake'. *The fact of the matter is that the extra letter yud actually does something concrete within the text.*

The Extraneous Yud Is A Point of Reference

The '*extraneous*' letter yud י serves as *a point of reference* pointing us to the place to begin looking for the revelations God has placed into the text.

---

[55]'Mene mene tekel upharsin' - Daniel interpreted these words (which were perhaps nouns for several weights or coins), which were written on the wall of Belshazzar's palace. They had baffled the wise men of Babylon (Dan. 5: 25–8). He claimed they meant 'to number', 'to weigh', 'to divide', adding up to a message of doom: the kingdom would shortly be divided between the Medes and the Persians. Encyclopedia.com

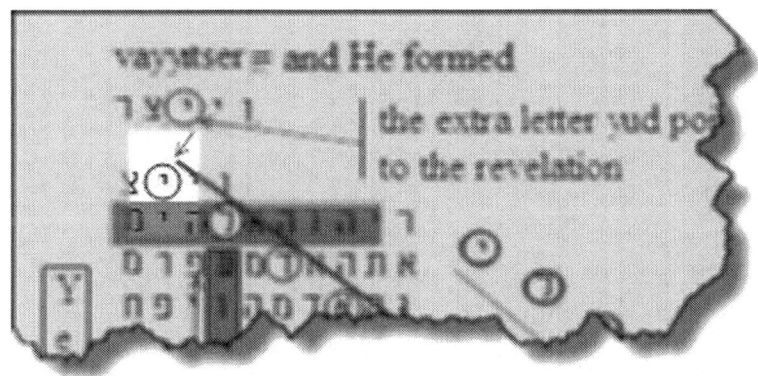

The '*extraneous*' yud also is the clue which points to the answer to the question which has been the primary focus of the division between Christians and Jews since the beginning of our historic and most tragic discord; namely, 'Is Yeshu, God, the Son?'; i.e., "Is Yeshua the only begotten Son of God, begotten of the Father before all worlds, God of God, Light of Light, very God of very God, begotten, not made, being of one substance with the Father"[56]It is now clear God the Father answers 'yes' to these questions.

We can now say with some level of certainty, if these two letters Yud found in our box aligned text, 'hint at anything at all', they most likely 'hint' not at the dual nature of the creation as was suggested by the ancient sages, but rather, they point to the dual nature of the Creator Himself; i.e., The Creator is Yeshua and is God - and God also chose to become one like unto us i.e., man.

In Summary, the word 'vayyitser' applied within the context of Genesis 2:7-8, when read literally, refers to the forming of human kind; yet, it obviously means much more than this. As we just mentioned, the word 'vayyitser' when decrypted is the clue which points to God's most Holy Mystery, it is the clue which reveals His Begotten Son.

---

[56] Nicene Creed

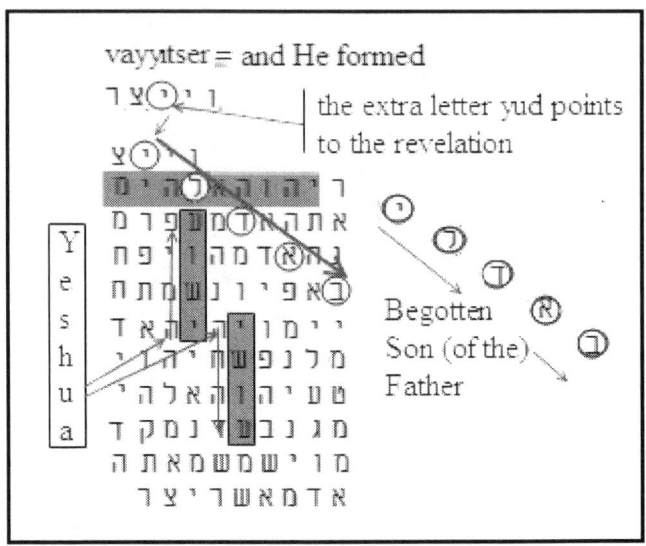

It's probably safe to say the most controversial title appended to the Name Yeshu is the title, 'God, the Son'.[57] So, we must ask if there is an indisputable encryption in the text which connects the phrase 'Begotten of the Father', the Person of Jesus and the Name Yahweh Elohim? And there is.

Note: The layout pattern you are about to see has already been introduced during the discussion regarding 'double lettering layouts patterns'. It is complex and the reader is urged to spend the time required to 'see this astounding, theologically rich, revelation which God has placed into His text.

In the following illustration, first locate the phrase 'yeleed ab – ילדאב', which means 'Begotten Son of the Father'. Notice also that this phrase is inextricably connected to God's Name, Yahweh Elohim, via the sharing of the Hebrew letter 'lamed ל. The next inextricable connection clearly links the phrase Begotten Son of the Father with the Name Yeshua, *which Name also begins with the extra letter yud contained in the misspelled word vayyitser* ו י י צ ר.

---

[57] This is quite different than saying 'son of God' in that all humans are sons and daughters of God

Since the term 'Son of the Father', the Name 'Yeshua' and the Name Yahweh Elohim are inextricably connected 'One to the Other' forevermore, Yeshu is, therefore revealed to be:

God, the Son, the Begotten of the Father!

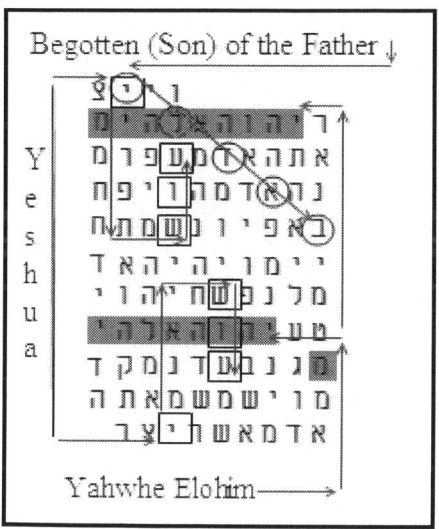

This title is not equal to the phrase 'Son of God' in that most believers, both Jew and gentile, believe all of us humans are sons and daughters of God. The main objection voiced concerning the title 'God the Son', being appended to the Person of Yeshua is that this title speaks of a 'consubstantial'[58] union between Yeshua and the Eternal - All Holy Being. Now, look a little deeper.

In the following illustration we see the 'Begotten (Son) of the Father' proceeding forth from Yahweh Elohim,[59] We also see the Name Yeshua being clearly identified as being the One, 'Who Is the Father's Son'. The manifestation of the human nature of the Fathers' Begotten

---

[58] As odd as this may sound to some readers, this means that in some sense the Substance which comprises the Person of the Father is identical to the Substance which comprises the Son i.e., the Substance of Divinity.
[59] Nicene Creed

Son Yeshua, is revealed via the shared letter dalet - ד contained in the word son i.e., - yeleed ילד.

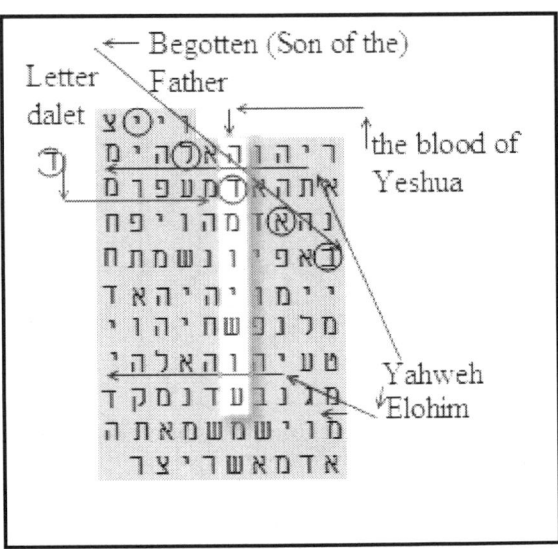

This letter clearly connects the phrase 'Begotten of the Father' to the phrase 'the blood of Yeshua' in that this letter is shared and is inextricable from either statement.

Put another way, we see the dogma that teaches – 'The Fathers Begotten Son, Yeshua, was in the flesh inextricably One within the Mystery of Yahweh Elohim, 'Divinity', upheld. The fact that the descendant spelling of Yeshua's Name is also seen to be inextricable from the Name Yahweh Elohim via the shared letter vav[60] only serves to strengthen this, God's Revelation.

For many, it is heresy to suggest that the Lord God has a Son i.e., One Who is of the same 'substance' as the Father. This is because if it were to be proven God has a 'begotten One' i.e., One who is of the same Divine Substance as God, what would logically result from this is the claim that there are multiple gods! After all, God's 'Substance is God'! So then, how is it possible for Christians

---

[60] Which pictorially means 'to nail'

to assert that 'Yeshu is con-substantial, i.e., of the same substance, with the Father and yet He is unique - all the while asserting there are not multiple gods'? Obviously, this is a paradox but as I will repeat many times more in this book, 'our God is a God of paradoxes'.

Until now - until seeing the revelation just seen - the teaching regarding the multiplicity of Persona within the singularity of Divinity, though an integral part of the Christian faith since the beginning, was most difficult to defend if we try to make our case by only using proof texts in the scripture. To do so, we must draw heavily upon the New Testament which is rejected by many critics. If we draw upon the Old Testament we do not see indisputable references in its text.

Therefore, until now we had to take this teaching regarding 'God, the Son' on faith. This teaching falls especially, quite short when played upon the ears of Jews and *non-Christians* who do not, as a norm, understand it to be referring to the internal *unity and the internal diversity* occurring within 'Godhead'. Of course no matter how fully theologians define the terms , 'Son of God', or 'Multiplicity of Persona within the singularity of Divinity', their efforts will lack precision and completeness in explaining the 'eternal and internal' 'Mystery Which is Divinity'.

I make this point because I don't want to spend time quibbling over terms and doctrines; rather, I'd much prefer to present God's revelation to you, the reader.

All that is required to affirm this teaching is to look at the above illustration of the biblical text and observe the revelation.

God, the Son

It is a plain and simple fact that God's decrypted revelations, as you have just seen, affirm He has a Holy and eternal Son. So, now we re-cap. The encrypted text refers to this Being as the 'son of the father', 'yeleed ab' – ילדאב. This phrase carries a *definite masculine inference* which can also be translated 'Boy (as in son) of the Father', hence,

'Begotten Son of the Father'.

No matter how' yeleed ab' – ילדאב is translated it definitively speaks of a parent / son relationship 'consubstantia'. A relationship in terms of co-mingled substance

It simply says, that God has a begotten Son; and, as you have just seen the phrase 'yeleed ab' – ילדאב refers to One Divine Person, His Name is Yeshua. A remarkable 'eye witness account' to the events of the New Covenant period comes from Yeshua's Jewish disciple John, called, 'The Theologian'. He says of Yeshua:

> In the origin[61] - (ἀρχῇ ,בְּרֵאשִׁית) - was the Word, and the Word was with God and the Word was God. The Same was in the origin - ἀρχῇ - with God. Jn1:1-2

> All things were made by Him; and without Him was not any thing made that was made. Jn1:3

Simply put, John was saying that the Creator is God, the Word. As we have mentioned earlier, before the creation, the Being we have come to know as Yeshua was with God and this Being is the Word of God. He is, was, and will eternally be, 'the paradoxical latent presence of change within the changeless'. He is the Begotten One, begotten of the Father'.[62]

---

[61] Refer to the discussion re: 'origins' in chapter 2.
[62] We'll speak more about this 'paradox' in a moment.

Chapter 7 - Consubstantial Relationship of the Son

Because the Genesis text itself can establish an inextricable unity between Yahweh Elohim and the One referred to as the 'begotten of the Father' i.e. the Creator, Yeshua, the *contextual relevancy* of the 'find' is absolutely astounding. This is so, both from a theological and a scientific, statistical perspective, precisely because Gen.2: 7-8 is a text entirely connected to God's act of creation!

There is zero possibility that such a laser sharp encryption could be found in such a contextually relevant text predating the known events of the disciple John's day. It is even more amazing when one considers the Genesis text predated John's life by almost two thousand years! It is absolutely obvious the Genesis encryptions had to have been deliberately inserted into the text by a Divine Being who clearly foreknew what would be happening during the days of Yeshu some two thousand years after the fact of their encryption. Such Omniscience is possible to God Alone. This is an important observation which has already been made, but is worth repeating here.

Because of the fact that God is revealing these encryptions to us, it is reasonable to conclude that, He is emphatically making a point; namely, He wants us to pay attention to what is being revealed. Less obvious but equally true, it can also be said God wants us to look even deeper into the revelation to ascertain if there is anything more which can be gleaned from it. And truly, there is a great deal more which can be seen in these revelations if only one were to look a little deeper.

For example, the phrase Begotten (Son) of the Father which we now understand is united to the Name Yahweh Elohim via the letter lamed – ל. This phrase reveals a deeper internal meaning which is 'hinted at' by the spacing of the letters which spell out the phrase itself. The lettering encryption pattern in this phrase is a simple diagonal ELS skip count of eight (8) letters i.e., there are five repeated skips of eight letters descending from the *extra letter yud* which spells the phrase Begotten of the Father. As just mentioned however, there is another encryption pattern which is pointed to by this diagonal eight count ELS pattern this other ELS encryption references Yeshua being the Boy of a woman,[63] whom we later see 'revealed' to be named Miriam i.e., Mary.

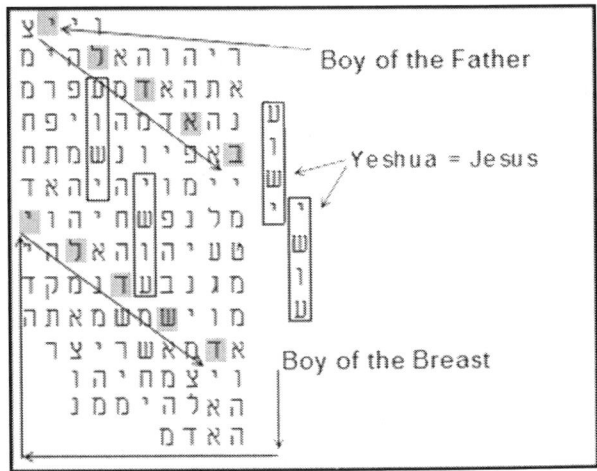

The meaning attached to the number eight is that of perfect completeness. God began His Sabbath rest on the seventh day and will establish His Perfect Kingdom upon the earth on *that day when He ceases His rest* i.e., the day outside of time, the eternal day of God, the 'dread and awesome' Day of the Lord. We'll discuss this further momentarily.

The Relevancy of the Surface Text

Returning to the subject of relevancy, Christians are taught without equivocation Yeshua is the Creator and God the Son; that He brings into existence all that exists. As you have just read, the Jewish Messianic exegete John reports in

---

[63] literally it says, 'boy of the breast' - a colloquial expression meaning the son of the woman whose 'breasts were nursed'

his gospel that Yeshua, the Word of God, brought all things into being and without Him was 'no thing' brought into the creation that exists within the creation. The relevancy of John's teaching to the surface text of Genesis is established in two ways:

1. the interconnected words and phrases which have revealed Yeshu as being precisely *that* Divine Being Who creates ex-nihilo[64]
2. the congruence of the inner textual details which unmistakably speak of the Creator, God, as being engaged in the very act of creating

Before we leave the subject of relevancy lets look a little deeper and see the other wonderful and *highly relevant teachings* God has placed into this text.

The Form of Yeshua

Next, we will see the Begotten of the Father is also identical with the One Who takes upon Himself עהשיומדה the 'form of Yeshua'

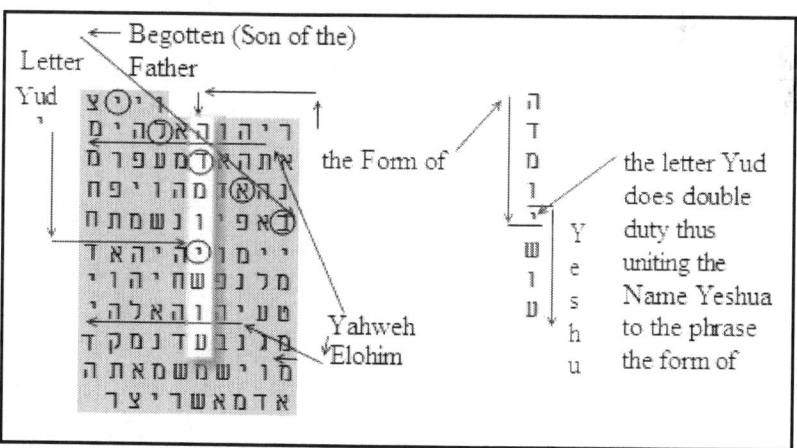

---

[64] Ex- ex-nihilo loosely means 'from nothing'

Spend a few moments, please, studying the above 'box aligned' revelation. The phrase 'the form of' and the Name 'Yeshua' are highlighted for you. There are several things to notice in the text; not the least of which is the intersecting of the term 'Begotten of the Father' with the phrase, 'the form of Yeshua'. The meaning of this inextricable connection is as profound as it is clear. God is revealing to us all that His 'Begotten Son' is He Who be-took upon Himself the 'Form of Yeshua'! It is important to understand the word 'form' sounds weaker to 'English ears' than it does to those who speak Hebrew. This word דמוי – the form of - conveys the 'sense' of 'identity', 'beingness', hence, 'ontology'. Put another way, the incarnated Yeshua is the 'Begotten Son of the Father' Who, when He was participating in the Form of Yeshua, "thought it not robbery to be equal with God" Philippians 2:6. Notice also, the phrases, 'the form of' and the Name 'Yeshua' share the letter 'yud' 'in common' and hence are to be considered inextricably one with each other because of it.

Looking at what is now being laid out in the text, we also note, the Holy One, the, 'Begotten of the Father' is now being 'graphically' revealed to be 'descending into the creation taking upon Himself the 'form of Yeshua'.

The Jewish Rabbi Paul (formerly called Saul)[65] expounds about this when he speaks of Yeshua and His earthly incarnation. Rabbi Paul says, He, "Yeshua: ..., made himself of no reputation, and took upon Him the form of a servant, and was made in the likeness of men", "and being found in the form of a man[66] He humbled Himself, having

---

[65] שָׁאוּל claimed to be "of the people of Israel, of the tribe of Benjamin, a Hebrew of Hebrews; in regard to the law, a Pharisee Phl. 3:5, also, "I am verily a man [which am] a Jew, born in Tarsus, [a city] in Cilicia, yet brought up in this city at the feet of Gamaliel, [and] taught according to the perfect manner of the law of the fathers, and was zealous toward God, as ye all are this day." Acts 22:3 Paul is responsible for bringing many gentiles into the worship of the God of Israel.

[66] i.e., the form of Yeshua

become obedient until death, even unto the death on a cross."
Philippians . 2:7-8

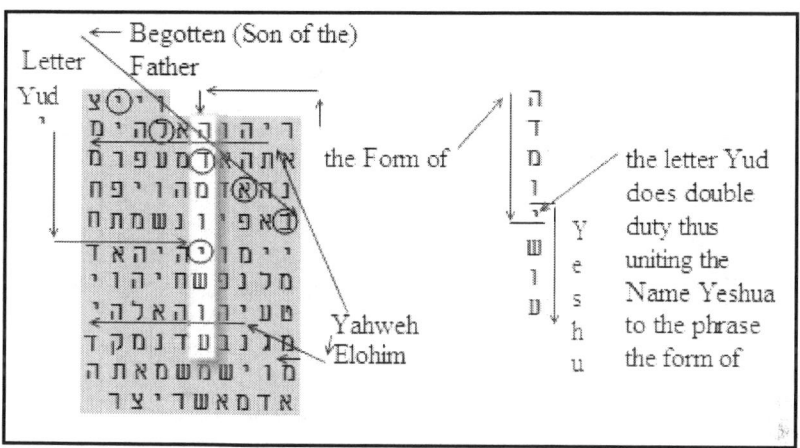

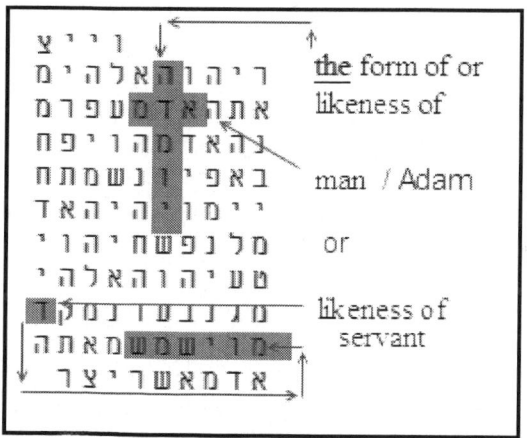

Having come this far, please spend a few moments
reviewing God's fuller revelation; bearing in mind, the
Father weaves patterns into other patterns using shapes,
shared letters, mirrored images as well as a misspelled word
to present His teaching regarding His only Begotten Son.

It is the 'Begotten of the Father' Whom we know to
be 'God, the man', in the form of Yeshua, the 'Second
Adam' Who "made himself of no reputation, and took upon

Himself the form of a servant, and was made in the likeness of men". It was Yeshua Who, "being found in the form of a man ..., humbled Himself, having become obedient until death, even unto the death on a cross." Philippians . 2:7-8

Deeper still. Notice that the central column of text contains a *dual* message. Reading the text letter by letter, top to bottom, we read, 'the blood of Yeshua, (Whom we already understand to be fully Man). It is His blood which is spilled upon the cross' (also revealed). But if we use the letter yud - ׳ - in a dual fashion we can extract the phrase 'the form of the servant, the man, Yeshua Who dies upon the cross.' We see further revealed that after all these things Yeshu is raised – קוּם - up from the dead!

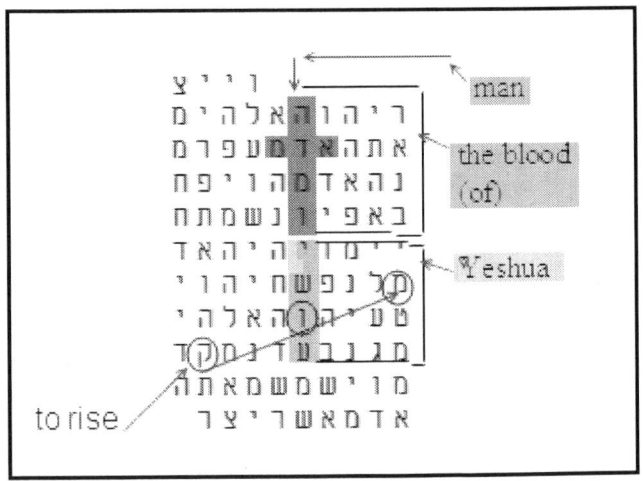

In this death we witness both His Humanity and His divinity. He died as do all humans. Yet, revealed in the image pattern of His crucifixion; we also learn it was the eternal Amen, Who is God Who was also, paradoxically, in the form of Yeshua, nailed to the cross. To see this amazing revelation, note that in the following illustration the spelling of the divine name 'Amen' *begins* with the letter aleph, א then proceeds diagonally to the left. (The letter hey – ה – simply means word 'the'). God's name, 'Amen', crosses over the phrase 'the blood of Yeshua' thereby connecting the Holy name 'Amen' to the incarnated God Yeshua. This is stunning!

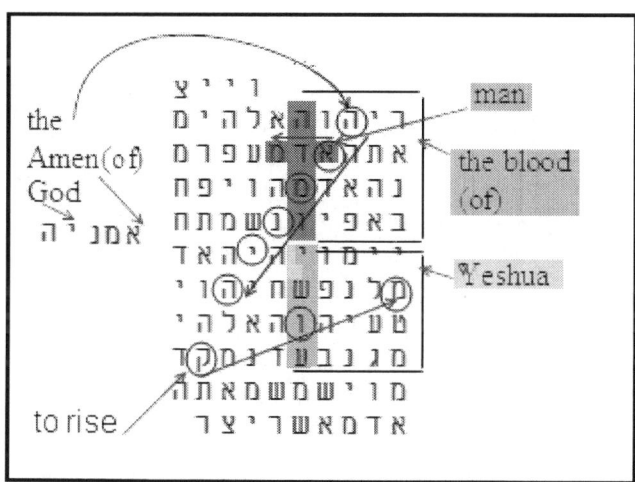

How thrilling it is to see clear evidence that what we have been taught is being revealed indisputably by God Himself, thus assuring us all that. 'in Yeshua, we too have the hope in our own resurrection'. To see all of these things please refer to the above few illustrations – as you can surmise the patterns interwoven upon other patterns becomes quite complex; yet, in these complexities we all can thrill to witnessing God's unraveling His teachings for us today.

Again, I'd like to stress these revelations are no mere chance happenings. They have obviously been put into the text by God on purpose. Once and for all, the very text of the Bible itself confirms by way of the most astounding revelations that God has a Holy and Divine Son.

The Jews and a Divine Messiah

I'd like to point out that although Yeshua's *Name* may not have been known to the Jewish faithful predating the time of Christ, there was within the Jewish camp a belief that God, the Creator, is also the forthcoming Messiah and obviously was pre-existent to the creation itself.[67]   Put another way,

The thought of a Divine Messiah is not novel to historic Judaism

I bring this point up because the majority of people reading this book might not know such is the case. The anti-Christian apologists in the Jewish camp go to great lengths to ensure that the very concept of a Divine Messiah is thoroughly discredited. They have gone so far as to redefine the notable suffering servant passages found in the scripture. *Never-the-less, predating Yeshua's day we encounter the thought of a Divine Messiah as being well established and well accepted, generally, even though not universally recognized.*[68]

To make this point, the following Jewish exegetical comments, though strange sounding to Christian ears, are illustrative. The fact remains, the concept, *the very concept itself,* of a Divine Messiah, did, most emphatically, exist in the time of Yeshua and the centuries preceding His advent and the centuries following His incarnation.

Indeed, R. Shim'on ben Laqish[69] unequivocally states,

'the spirit of God hovering over the face of the deep in Genesis 1 ff., is None other than the spirit of King

---

[67] Genesis Rabbah 1:4 refers to Messiah as one of Six pre-creation existences bearing the very Image of Yahweh having arisen within the unfathomable Depths of Divinity

[68] It only became novel as the polemic between Jews and Christians intensified after Yeshua's advent.

[69] He was regarded as one of the most prominent amoraim of the third century. *Amora* אמורא; "those who say" or "those who tell over"), were renowned Jewish scholars who "said" or "told over" the teachings of the Oral law, from about 200 to 500 CE. Wiki. R. Shim'on ben Laqish.

Messiah'.[70]

This well respected Jewish exegete refers to Messiah as being the Creator! This is a critical observation because anti-Yeshuan apologists vehemently maintain that such a thought i.e., a Messiah Who is God, is not part of historic Judaism. They have beguiled their people and have kept the reality which God is revealing to us today hidden from view.

Consider as well what the widely quoted Jewish sage and scholar R. Simeon ben Yochai[71] who writes the following lines thus putting to rest most arguments as to what *historic* Judaism teaches regarding the divinity of Messiah. He says:

> "There is a Perfect Man who is an Angel. This Angel is Metatron, the keeper of Israel; He is man in the Image of the Holy One, blessed be He, Who is an Emanation from Him; yea, **He is Yahweh**, of Him it cannot be said, He is created, formed or made; but He is the *Emanation* from God. This agrees exactly with what is written, Jeremiah 23:5-6 about David's Branch that though He shall be Perfect Man, yet He is, "Lord our righteousness". [72]

At first glance, the manner in which the Jewish sages describes the Divinity of Messiah may not seem to fit with traditional, 'orthodox', Christian teaching; however, upon a more careful reading of the text it actually agrees more with our teaching than it disagrees with it.[73]

---

[70] The Babylonian Talmud too states Messiah was One of seven pre-creation Existences and that His Name will endure forever.

[71] He was a very important first century rabbi and exegete. His writings are universally quoted by Jewish scholars and students as being authoritative.

[72] The Propositions of the Zohar, cap. 38, Amsterdam ed.

[73] The Name Metatron may 'throw' the reader, but it is a Name frequently assigned by Jewish mystics to a Divinity which, for all practical purposes, seems to resemble the Person Christians refer to as

In summary, what the sage is saying in his text certainly *proves* that 'the concept of a Divine Messiah' has historically been an accepted Jewish teaching and is most assuredly, not a novel idea. The only unaddressed question, up to this point in history, is the *identity of this Messiah*; and, God Himself is now putting that question to rest. Clearly His Name is Yeshua. Prior to the revelations God is making known to us today, He provided several clues to enable His people to identify His Messiah when He arrives. We'll next consider a few of these teachings.

Messiah 'The Righteous Branch'
Here is the text R. Simeon ben Yochai was referencing when he said ..., "about David's Branch that though He shall be Perfect Man, yet He is, "Lord our righteousness".:

> "Behold, the days come, saith the LORD, that I will raise unto David a righteous Branch, and a King shall reign and prosper, and shall execute judgment and justice in the earth. In his days Judah shall be saved, and Israel shall dwell safely: and this [is] his Name whereby he shall be called, THE LORD OUR RIGHTEOUSNESS." Jeremiah 23:5-6

As we go through this discussion, keep in mind that in both Jewish and Christian camps, the Righteous Branch spoken of by the prophets is understood to be the Messiah of Israel. Our question is, 'is there a connection to be found in Genesis 2:7-8 which ontologically links the Yeshua to the Personage called 'The Righteous Branch' discussed in prophecy? To answer this question we first need to understand 'The Righteous Branch' is a title given to the

---

the 'Word of God'. The term 'emanation' may be understood as 'The proceeding One' and the rest of the sages statement needs no further elaboration. It perfectly matches the teachings found in the teachings of the ancient Christians.

biologic, genetic, hence, ontological family line of 'Jesse', the grandson of Boaz and Ruth. Jesse is the father of David, the king and the great, great, great, ancestor of Jesus, Yeshua. The prophet Isaiah refers to Messiah's familial lineage this way.

> And in that day there shall be a **root** of Jesse, which shall stand for an ensign of the people; to it shall the Gentiles seek and his rest shall be glorious Is. 11:10

Isaiah's choice of words clearly requires a 'direct', ontological unity between Yeshua and Jesse. It works this way. King David is the 'root of Jesse' and the 'Righteous Branch' i.e., Messiah i.e., Yeshua, spoken of by Jeremiah, is the distant 'blood related', great grandson of King David. Hence, there is an inextricable blood unity between Jesse, King David and Messiah.

Anointed One And Messiah

Looking at Isaiah's and Jeremiah's prophecies, there are 8 attributes attributed to Messiah, God's Anointed One. Each of these are amazingly found deeply encrypted into the text of Gen.2:7-8. The question is this, 'will the box aligned text' also show these attributes to being in some manner clearly attached to the Name Yeshua?' Obviously the answer to this question is yes!

1. in His day the House of Judah will be saved
2. He is inextricably connected to Jesse i.e., Jesse's root
3. He is the 'Righteous Branch'
4. Messiah's birth from a virgin will be known as the ensign or sign
5. To Him will the gentiles seek
6. His rest will be considered glorious
7. each prophecy refers to the Person of Messiah
8. elsewhere, each considers Messiah to be 'Anointed'

Let's go through each of these attributions and see the remarkable ways God encrypted them into Genesis 2:7-8.

1. In His day the House of Judah will be saved.

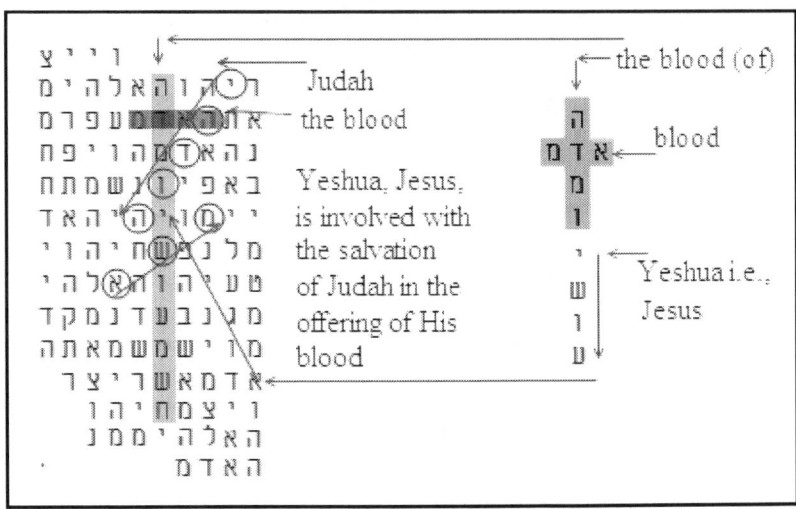

We are taught that in the sacrifice worked out upon the cross, in the shedding of Yeshua's blood as the guilt offering, the house of Judah i.e., the house of the Jews began to enjoy the mystery of salvation by faith

2. Messiah, Yeshua i.e., Jesus is inextricably connected to Jesse i.e., in Jesse's bloodline.

3. Messiah, Yeshua, Jesus, is the 'Righteous Branch'. (See our discussion below for the regarding the revelation of the branch, the pehsech)

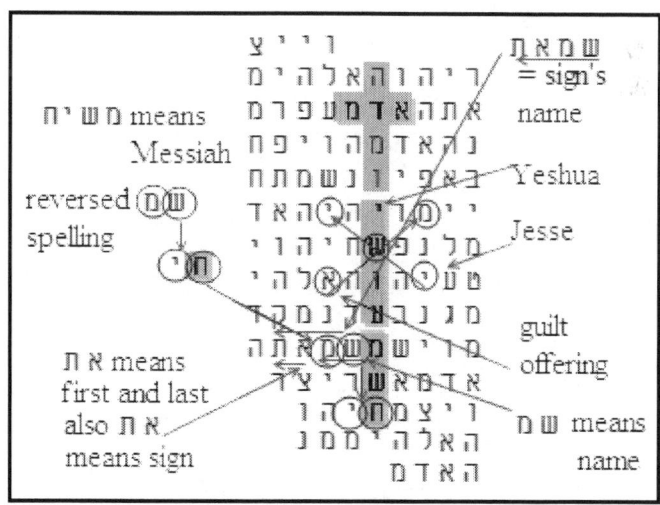

4. Messiah's birth from a virgin will be known as the ensign or sign.

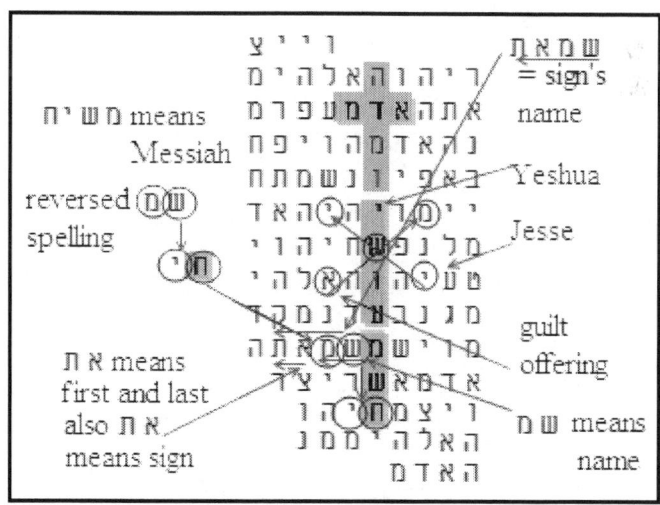

As you can see the illustration is becoming increasingly

complicated, so it may take a few moments to work our way through it. Still, it is very much worth the effort. In the above illustration, we are reading a phrase containing the word 'sign'. What is so special about this word is the fact that Isaiah considers the One who is the 'sign' or ensign' to be the Messiah. Followers of Yeshua, also, have from the beginning, understood Isaiah's prophecy to refer directly to the Person of Messiah – Whom they confess to be Yeshua, Isaiah's prophesized 'sign'. About this sign, Isaiah says it will consist of a 'virgin giving birth' i.e., a virgin mother'. The One, so born to her, the virgin, is identified by the prophet as the long awaited Messiah, the sign.

To decrypt this revelation we consider that the Hebrew word for sign את - is adjacent to the Hebrew word for Name שם. This word arrangement is asking for the 'Name of the sign' i.e., the 'name of the woman', Messiah's 'virgin mother'.

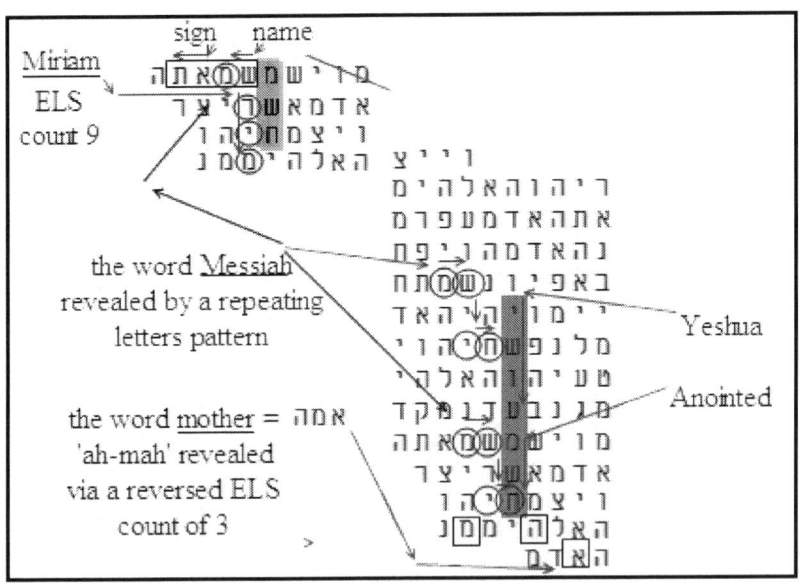

Obviously, it is well known and universally accepted the name of Yeshua's mother is Mary i.e., in Hebrew it is Miriam – מרים. Our question now becomes, "is Mary the 'sign' spoken about; if so, can we see revealed in the text that she enjoys some inextricable connection with the Messiah? Also, can we find in the text a revelation which connects Mary's Son, Yeshua, to herself and Isaiah's prophecy?" If all this can be done we will be correct to assert that Mary is the 'virgin mother' spoken about in Isaiah's prophecy.

A very careful examination of the above two illustrations can certainly reveal that Mary is the 'virgin mother of Yeshua' , 'God's Anointed Messiah'. And because she is the mother of Messiah she therefore must also be a 'virgin', at least this is so, according to the prophecy. Also adjacent to the Hebrew letter Mem – מ, the first letter of Miriam's Name are the letters aleph and tav – את -which letters can convey the meaning 'sign'. Another meaning attached to the adjacent Hebrew letters, aleph and tav – את - is 'beginning and end' or 'first and last'. If this meaning were translated into the Greek language, then we would understand the meaning to be 'alpha and omega'. Any one conversant with the biblical text will quickly understand these references point directly to the Messiah and Creator respectively. So once again, the contextual relevancy of the revealed encryptions we are seeing in the box aligned text is stunningly evident.

5. To Messiah will the gentiles seek.

> The group of disciples of Yeshua though starting out mainly to be Jewish, quickly changed into being mainly gentiles. This happened as friction increased between the Jewish disciples of Yeshua and Jews antagonistic to Yeshua. By the end of the first century the evangelizing work of the then still living Jewish disciples was centered directed toward the Jew first, then the gentile. Their efforsts became complicated primarily due to the Roman sponsored 'forced relocations' of the Jewish populations of the middle east resulting in   vast numbers of gentiles

being brought into the fold of the Jewish believers in Yeshua.

6. His rest will be considered glorious.

In Messianic circles the rest spoken of by Isaiah points to mystery of the cross, the tomb, the resurrection from the dead i.e., the truly glorious, unfathomably, Holy Mystery of Salvation in which Yeshua first, and, in Him and through Him, all mankind can now come to rest eternally in the 'Bosom of Abraham' i.e., the Father. (Each of these things too are encrypted into text of Genesis 2:7-8 although they are spoken about elsewhere in this book.)

7. The prophets, Isaiah and Jeremiah, are each referring to the attributes of the Person of Messiah.

(We have already seen the revelation where Yeshua's Name is clearly connected to the word Messiah – nothing can be more clear than this!)

8. Elsewhere, each considers Messiah to be 'Anointed'.

We have already seen the revelation where Yeshua's Name is clearly connected to the word Anointed. (Again, nothing can be more clear than this!)

Weaving each of these revelations together we begin to see an amazing agreement within the teachings of both the old and the new testaments connecting the Old Testament to the New Testament. This agreement thus reveals 'one complete Book' i.e., a beautiful complimentary story. Also, hopefully, these things will help to bridge the gap between Judaism and Christianity revealing each to be complimentary and *essential to the other. At* least this is so in terms of a completed faith system. Judaism is fulfilled in Christianity and Christianity is completed only by virtue of Judaism. Each is inextricably one within the other and to extract one from the other is to destroy both!

We can now 'visually' 'connect the dots' in this emerging teaching. Yeshua was the 'blood relative' of both Jesse; and by virtue of this fact, He is also connected to David's bloodline, hence, Yeshua is, also of the 'House of Judah'. Amazingly this fact is also attested to in God's revelation.

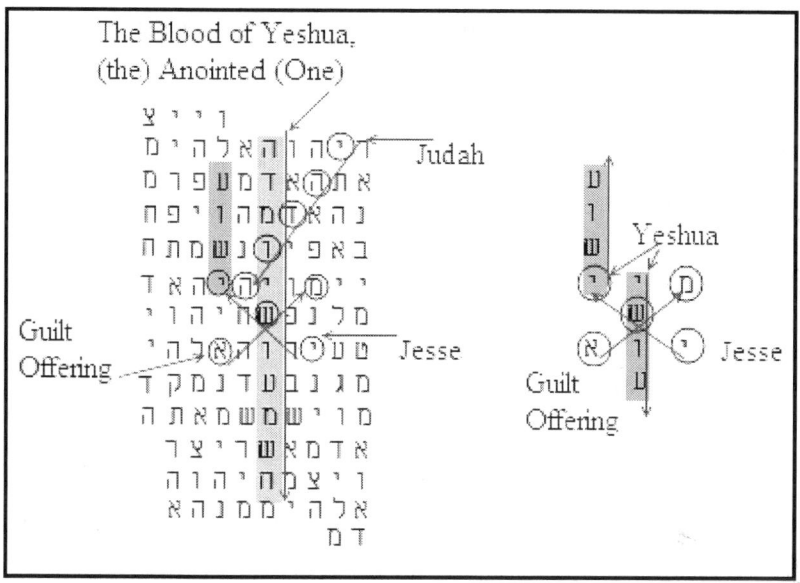

So, how is Judah to be saved in the days of Messiah's earthly walk? Judah is 'saved' in terms of its restoration into spiritual fellowship with the Father via the atoning sacrifice accomplished in the guilt offering in the spilling of Yeshua's' blood upon the altar of the cross. This is to say, Yeshua became Judah's eternal sacrificial offering for sin in the shedding of His blood. Yeshua became Judah's everlasting 'guilt offering', its Asham.

A wonderful deepening of the revelation is seen when we note that the Name Judah is inextricably connected to the phrase 'the form of Yeshua' via the shared letter Vav .

Considering the pictographic meaning connected to the letter Vav - ו i.e., to nail or affix by pinning or nailing, we can interpret the encrypted text as follows: 'The form of Yeshua' is 'pinned' to the house of Judah'.

To Jewish ears, this statement points in a direction different than what gentiles might think. It points to the teaching of the bondservant. It says Yeshua has voluntarily become the 'bond servant to Judah (see the discussion regarding the 'bond servant', below).

> Let this mind be in you which was also in Messiah Yeshua, who, being in the form of God, did not consider it robbery to be equal with God, but made Himself of no reputation, taking the form of a **bondservant**, and coming in the likeness of men. And being found in appearance as a man, He humbled Himself and became obedient to the point of death, even the death of the cross. Philip.2:5-11

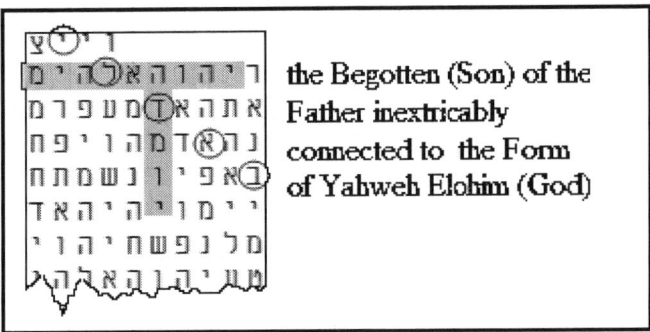

the Begotten (Son) of the Father inextricably connected to the Form of Yahweh Elohim (God)

Make no mistake when reading over these teachings, God is revealing that it is His Begotten Son Yeshua Who is doing all of this. Yeshua, Jesus, is inextricably united within Yahweh Elohim, God, and is the Begotten One of the Father. It is therefore God Who takes on the form of a servant i.e., Yeshua Who is 'pinned' to the house of Judah thus by becoming its 'bondservant'. Please spend sufficient time to fully absorb what is being revealed in the following two illustrations.

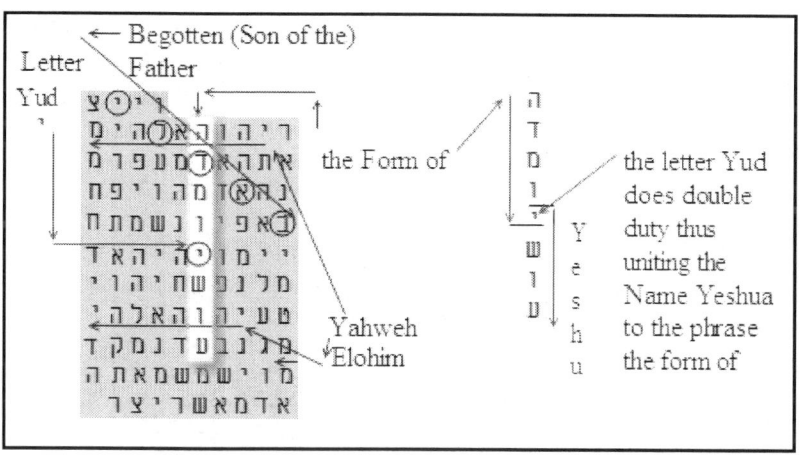

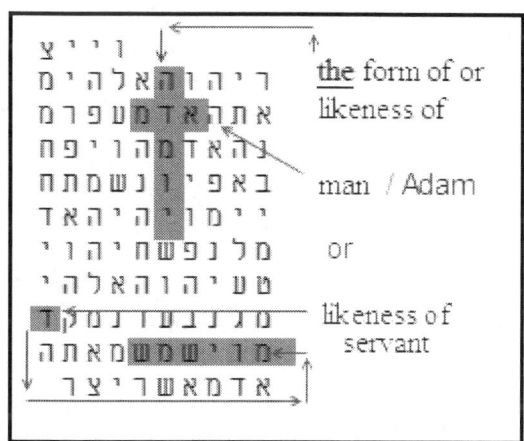

The Bondservant

In Judaism when one does not desire to leave the servitude of another or voluntarily desires to be the bond servant of another the 'other' pins or pierces with an awl the ear lobe of the bondservant to the *doorpost of the house*, - spilling blood upon the doorpost, preparatory to putting a gold ring through the wound which indicates the wearer of the earring as the 'bondservant'. From that moment onward, the 'bondservant' is the owner's property. He is obedient to the master, doing his masters will and resides under his master's protection. By way of comparison, the night before

He was crucified, Yeshua exemplified the true obedient nature of the bondservant when He expressed His willingness to obey the Father ..., even unto His death, a death upon the cross.

> ....,"He went away again the second time, and
> prayed, saying, O my Father, if this cup may not pass
> away from me, except I drink it, thy will be done."
> Matt.26:42

Theologically, the idea of blood spilling upon the door post of the house is compelling. It speaks to the ideas of Passover, salvation, covenant relationship and deliverance i.e., escaping the consequences of God's wrath via the spilling of the lamb's blood upon the wooden altar of the doorpost of the home. That the Person of Yeshua is connected with the bondservant in this remarkably short encryption is quite astounding. It is precisely His total submission to the Fathers Will, even onto a dreadful death upon the cross, that the 'Lamb of God' confronted the spilling of His blood upon the dreadful altar of the cross. His obedience to the Father as 'the bondservant' overturned the ancient disobedience of Adam thus-by ushering into the creation the full reconciliation between God and man.

It becomes even more astounding when we realize the encrypted text also reveals the terms 'guilt offering' and the name Jesse to be part of this same teaching. We see clearly revealed that the great grandson of Jesse i.e., Yeshu, became humanity's 'bondservant' 'saving' Judah in His Own day by offering Himself as the 'guilt offering', the Asham אשמ', via the shedding of His Own precious blood.

As mentioned before, that Yeshu is '*that* Righteous Branch' sprouting from the root of Jesse makes it especially interesting that another 'branch type word' is to be found in the text. The word which intersects with the name Yeshua is pehsech פשח [74]; and means, 'that particular branch which is split off from the tree'. The rabbis have in the past been asked, 'what does one do with a branch that splits off from the tree which is not completely severed from the root and still remains alive in the rootstock 'on the Sabbath - the Lords mandated day of rest'? Remember, Yeshu was crucified during the period of the Great Sabbath, The rabbinic teaching is that a split off branch is to be bound to the tree if the injury occurs during the Sabbath rest which is the 'Lords day'– not for the purpose that it is to grow back into the tree[75] but so that no further harm to the tree is done. Such a branch remains part of the tree – alive in the tree, yet it is differentiated from the tree at the point of the split. Yeshu is prefigured in this rabbinic image. He is that branch, separated from the tree of 'legalistic Judaism' but never-the-less, Yeshua, 'the branch' is always alive and one with 'true Judaism' – bound to it and inextricable from it, forever one with His Jewish roots and His great 'forefather Jesse.

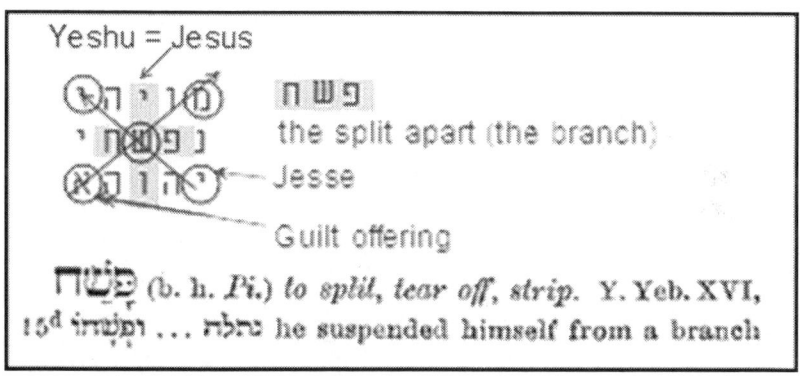

God's Corroboration Of These Things Found In The Text Of Jeremiah 23:6

It might be interesting to the reader to know God also corroborates what I have just said by having encrypted into the text of Jeremiah 23:6 (previously mentioned) both the

---

[74] פשח Targum on I Sam. XV, 33 regarding branches which are split off.
[75] Which would constitute labor on the 'Lords Day'

Name Yeshu and an image of a cross (Yeshu's death upon the cross ushered in, according to Christian Theology, the 'great Sabbath rest' of the Lord).

```
בימיו תושע יהודה וישראל ישכן      ׳ מ ׳ ב
לבטח וזה־שמו אשר־יקראו יהוה      ו ת ש ו ע ה
צדקנו :                       ו ד ה ׳ ו ש ר
                              ל כ ש ׳ ל א
In his days Judah shall be saved, and Israel shall    ב ח ט ו ו ה ש
dwell safely; and this is his name whereby he shall    מ ו א ר ש ׳ ק
be called, The LORD is our righteousness.    ו א ר ו ׳ ה ה
Jeremiah 23:6                        צ ד ק נ ו
```

Yeshua's death upon the cross also began the great mystery of the salvation of Judah and all mankind thus He is called the Lord, (Yahweh), our Righteousness. Here is Jeremiah's text presented both in the regular way and box aligned fashion.

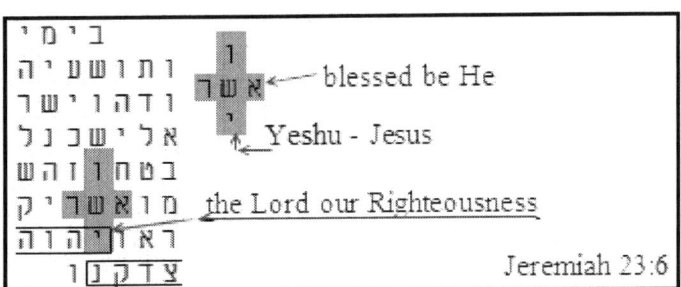

```
                                    Jeremiah 23:6
```

blessed be He

Yeshu - Jesus

the Lord our Righteousness

The above illustration, is the Divinely encrypted revealed teaching which is highlighted and annotated for your ease of study. It is obvious, the Name Yeshu and His work of salvation upon the cross are even referred to deep within the great *Messianic prophecy* of Jeremiah previously mentioned as being quoted by rabbi Simeon ben Yochi. The full revelation contained in the cross pattern states 'Yeshu, Blessed be He, '(the) Lord our Righteousness''. Yeshu's Name and the phrase '(the) Lord our Righteousness are inextricably, hence ontologically, connected to each other via the sharing of the Hebrew letter - ׳ – yud in both the Names Yeshu and Yahweh i.e., Lord. If one were to combine all of the concepts revealed in Jeremiah's 'box aligned' prophecy we can easily read: 'Yeshu, blessed be He (the crucified One), (the) Lord (Yahweh), our Righteousness[76]

Back To Our Text - The God Man

Many people find the idea of a God Man hard to accept. So, rather than turning to complex arguments we can instead observe a rather amazing revelation from God Himself, the Author of the text. He makes an indisputable point via His encryption of a 'design pattern' which he repeats four times in our 'box aligned text. This one may require some effort to see. The revelation takes the shape of four triangles. Each triangle reveals Yeshua to be inextricably One within Yahweh

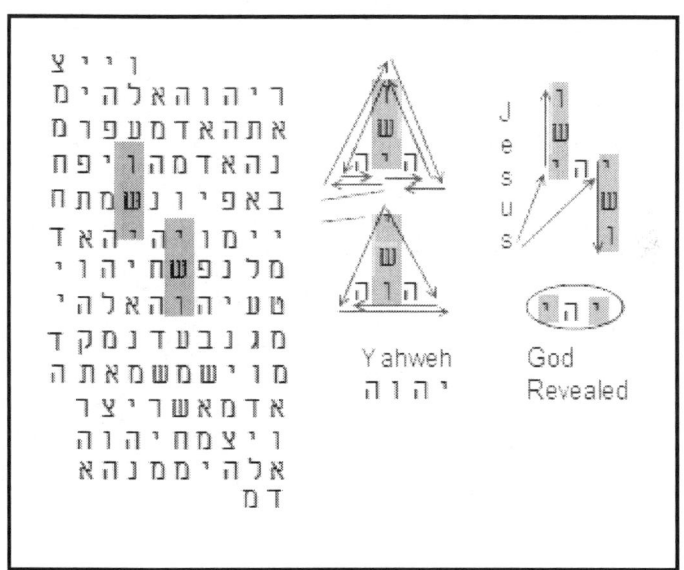

---

[76] It is indeed interesting how frequently we see Yeshua's Inextricably connected to Yahweh's Name via the Hebrew letter yud.

In every case, the revelation begins with the letter Yud ׳. It is this letter which begins the Hebrew spelling of the Names Yahweh and Jesus. Following the directions of the arrows in the illustrated pattern, the reader will quickly see that at each angle of the triangle pattern is the sequentially correct letter spelling God's sacred Name, Yahweh. Each triangle is presented in forward and reversed order making a total of four triangles. Each spelling of the Name Yahweh begins within the spelling of the Name Jesus, i.e., Yeshu.

Deepening the incredulity of this observation is the fact that God chose to embed these revelations into the text linking them to each other by a pictogram which states 'God Revealed' and uniting His Name to the Name Yeshu. This revelation is so incredible that little else can be said than what has just been said.

The Blood of Yeshua

The Divine plan for the human incarnation of Yeshua and His voluntary sacrifice upon the cross emanates (proceeds) out from deep within The Holy Will of the Lord God.[77] This plan finds its formation within the abode of eternity but its manifestation within the confining limits of the creation itself (His Own creation)! The Divine Yeshua springs forth from the human root of Jesse thereby, revealing Him to be, in the words of rabbi Simeon ben Yochai,

> "... (the) man in the Image of the Holy One, blessed be He, Who is an Emanation from Him; yea, *He is Yahweh*, of Him it cannot be said, He is created, formed or made; but He is the Emanation from God."[78]

We can add to the rabbi's thought that the Christian

---

[77] Nicene Creed
[78] R. Simeon ben Yochai

teaching that Yeshua's incarnation was Divinely purposed in order that He would make perfect atonement (the guilt offering) for mankind in the spilling of His Own blood.

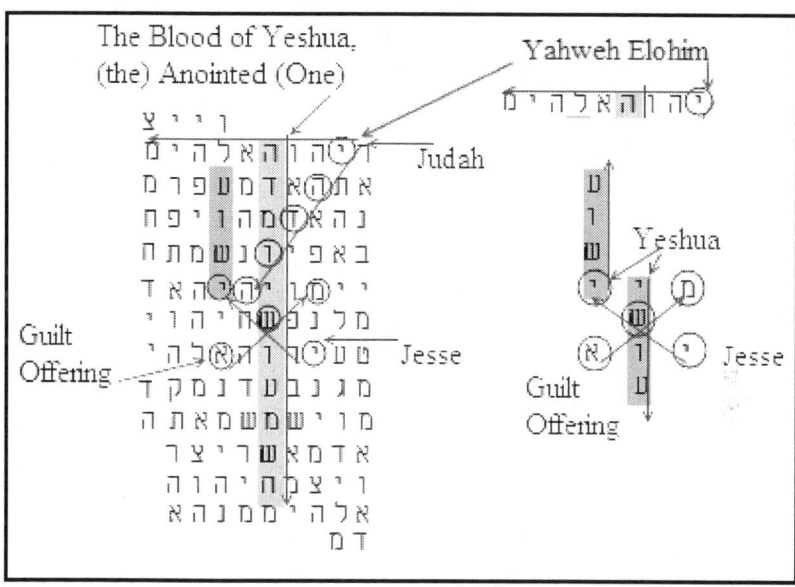

We need to keep in mind that the offering of blood is an essential part of the offering which atones for guilt.

The Suffering Messiah

So why would God 'purpose' His Only Begotten Son to be offered as the guilt offering and suffer death, even death upon the cross?

The prophet Isaiah says the Messiah will be 'crushed (so) that His Soul might be offered in restitution, (a guilt offering). Isaiah states the purpose behind the offering is to see if God's servant, Yeshua, would be *willing* to do this in obedience to the Father.

How marvelous it is that God encrypts His Sons Name into the text of Isaiah 53:10 just has He has done every where one cares to look in the Bible. It seems wherever one expects to see Yeshu's, Jesus', Name in the Bible, there it is. For example the Isaiah text just mentioned has the following encryption which displays Yeshu's Name

87

crossed over by the phrase 'guilt offering' and then doubly 'criss crossed ' over by a Hebrew term which stands for a Name of God!

Without a doubt God reveals Yeshu to be His guilt offering and reveals Him to be the bearer of the Name universally accepted by the Jews to refer to God alone i.e., HaShem.

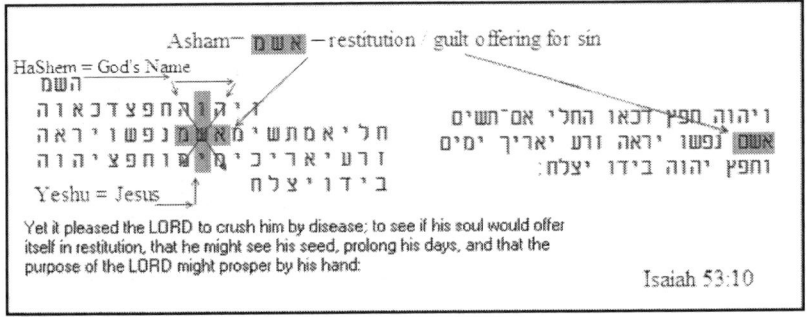

The actual word used by the prophet Isaiah in describing mode of death Yeshu was to endure is, 'Asham' אשמ which means *guilt offering*; and, obviously we see this word, אשמ, in the cross image which is formed in Isaiah's prophecy as the phrase 'guilt offering crosses over the Hebrew Name 'Yeshu', Jesus..

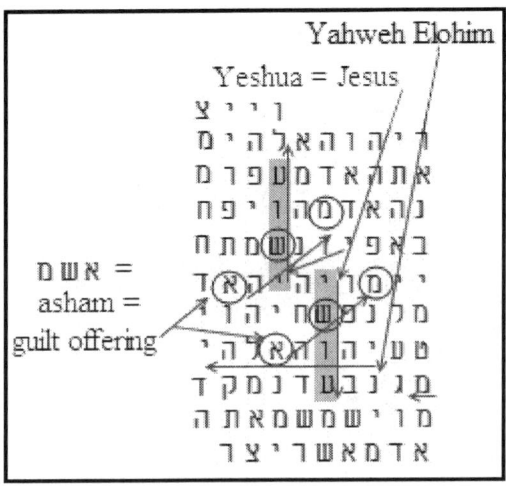

We also now realize it is not coincidental to see the word 'Asham' – guilt offering' twice in the Genesis text under consideration (below). Each time it is found it also intersects with Jesus' Hebrew Name, Yeshua and once with the phrase Yahweh Elohim thus indicating that from deep within eternity itself, Yeshua was always intended to be the guilt offering – a purpose which He accomplished within the creation, yet remaining inextricably One within Yahweh Elohim!.

The Hidden Things Which Thou Didst Not Know

So we now see Yeshua involved in the 'offering of His soul in restitution' exactly as spoken about by the prophet Isaiah. (We'll cover the teachings of Isaiah and the dozens of amazing revelations God encrypted in Isaiah's prophecy in a later book.)

Sometimes, we hear an objection, 'that if Yeshua were Messiah where is the temple? Where is the sacrificial Lamb? Some want to say both are required to be in place in the day of Messiah. However, by now you have probably realized Yeshua, Himself is the Temple and He, Himself is the blood sacrifice. Compare this teaching with what is contained in the Jewish commentary regarding Exodus 32:32[79]

> *Moses spake before the Holy One, blessed be He, "will not a time come when Israel have neither tabernacle nor temple? What will happen to these people as regards atonement?" The Holy One, blessed be He, replied, " I will take a righteous man from amongst them and make Him a pledge on their account, and I will atone for their iniquities."[80]*

---

[79] Torah Rabbahs, John Boylan, M/Div., Exodus Rabbah. 2005
[80] Everymans Talmud. Abraham Cohen. 1949, Schocken Books, p.118

Again, taking a deeper look into this wonderful Isaiah revelation, we learn about the 'righteous man' just spoken about in the commentary. Yeshu, Jesus, is the One referred to as the 'Asham' – the guilt offering - and He is also the One identified as HaShem i.e., 'the Name' (of God). It is He Who is the subject of the sage's commentary on Ex. 32:32.

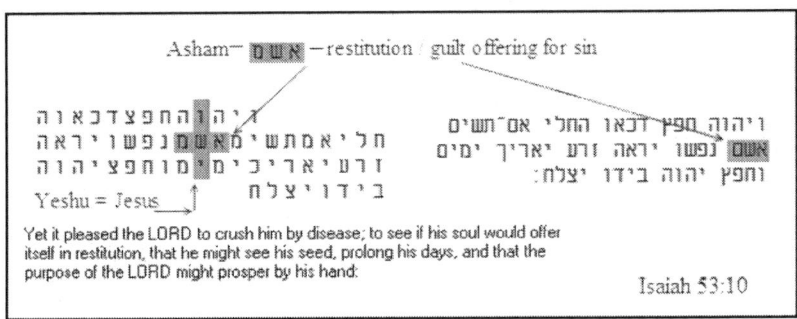

Yet it pleased the LORD to crush him by disease; to see if his soul would offer itself in restitution, that he might see his seed, prolong his days, and that the purpose of the LORD might prosper by his hand:

Isaiah 53:10

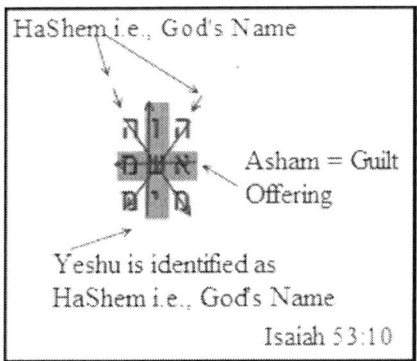

The Lord wanted to see if the second perfect man, the Second Adam, Yeshu, might be perfectly obedient and trust *in the Will of the Father.* He united Himself into our universal plight by paradoxically doing a thing in which it is impossible for God to Do i.e., agreeing unto His Own death. In this condition He became very much like all of us. He agreed that if it is the Fathers will, He would die. He thus-by joined Himself into our misery so that through His 'obedient' death He began the process of restoration, on behalf of all of us, unto the Father. He became for us, the 'Lord our

Righteousness', Who does not lie and Who taught us that in trusting Him we are through Him restored unto the Father.

Consider this fact the next time you might be tempted to ask 'why does God allow me to suffer. God knew Yeshu would suffer agonizingly before He made you or me. Yet He loved us enough to create us even though it meant He would suffer to do so. He foreknew that ushering us into paradise meant Him ushering Himself into our common end, Sheol i.e., death – (and that when He arose up from death, we who share the common grave with Him might be raised up to life eternal). He suffered first that we might suffer no more.

In summary, encrypted in the text of the suffering servant prophecy by Isaiah we see centrally encrypted the Name of Jesus and the word 'guilt offering Asham - אשם ' both words being aligned in such a way as to form the shape of a cross. Seemingly so as to leave no stone unturned as to what God is revealing here, we also see the word HaShem השם which has the unique meaning in Judaism to refer exclusively to God Almighty. The word HaShem incredibly is imposed into the revelation in a pattern I refer to as an 'x marks the spot pattern'. We see nine letters, embedded in a Messianic text, which when 'box aligned', has each letter being incorporated into an revelation speaking to millennia old teachings regarding the suffering servant, Messiah, Yeshu, Jesus.

This is but a quick excursion into the prophecy of Isaiah. A much fuller exposition is to be found in a forthcoming book.

I needed to draw upon Isaiah because we find the same terminology in the verses of Gen. 2:7-8. The exact word used in the prophecy of Isaiah is the word twice encrypted into our text. The word is 'Asham' – אשם' meaning 'guilt offering'.

Yeshua Is Revealed To Be 'The Acceptable Guilt Offering'

Since God is revealing Yeshua to be the Guilt Offering it must follow Yeshua is the acceptable Guilt Offering for the sins of mankind. This teaching is exactly the same as revealed in Christian teaching. The thrust of this teaching is also exactly what the prophet Isaiah foretold in his great Messianic prophecies.

We now know Yeshua is One within the Father - consubstantial and of One Essence with Divinity. Yeshua is the Asham אשמ of God and is God - a fact clearly displayed in the mirrored image pattern found in the box aligned text.

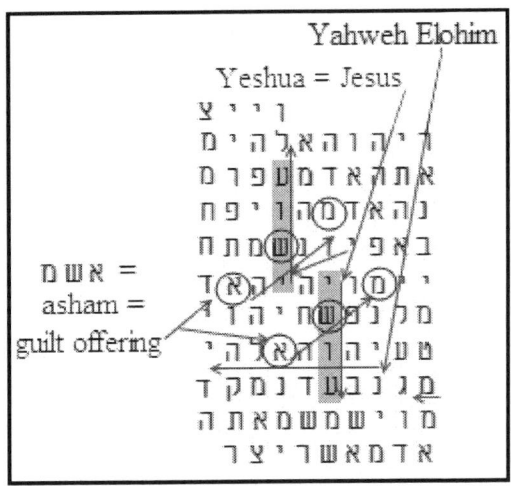

Notable also is the fact that both findings of the word Asham i.e., guilt offering are inextricably connected to the Name Yeshua and are patterned into text as exact duplicate images. Moreover, each revelation of the word Asham crosses over the Name Yeshua at the Hebrew letter Shin, ש, which has, itself, a clear theological meaning in Judaism.

"The secret of the *shin* is "the flame bound to the coal [Divine Essence]." A simmering coal actually possesses an invisible flame within it, which

emerges and ascends from the surface of the coal when the coal is blown upon…., the inner flame is the 'paradoxical latent presence of the power of change' within the changeless. The outer flame of the *shin* is continuously in a state of motion and change."
Gal Einai Website

About this teaching, one can quickly see several analogies and make the connections between the ancient teachings regarding Yeshua and His relationship within the eternal Divine Mystery of Godhead and what is being said about the Hebrew letter shin regarding the hidden flame which is in the coal and which is perfectly of one nature with it. Both the flame and the coal are one, undivided of one nature and yet each is differentiated from the other in its characteristics and unique properties.

Yeshua Is Revealed To Be The One Called HaShem

The word HaShem simply means, 'the Name'. Interestingly, it is not found even one time in the entirety of scripture being used in the manner Jews use it today i.e., to directly refer to God.

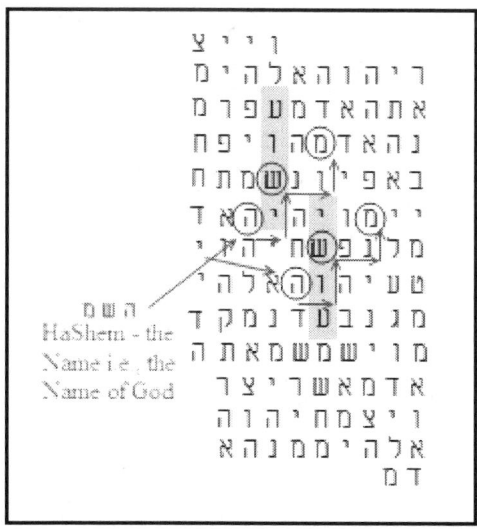

HaShem – the Name i.e. the Name of God

Yet in the box aligned text Yahweh Elohim is identifying the personage to Whom this word correctly attaches. It is attached to Yeshua. An aside: of particular note regarding this revelation is the fact that a typical ELS bible code type search would never pick up this significant revelation since the pattern in the text is a repeating 'design or layout' pattern and is not to be found in equidistant spaced letters.

Again, completing the revelation is the Hebrew letter shin ש just spoken about (above). It is this letter, shin, which mystically defines what is transpiring in the depths of God's Being. It is the Hebrew letter shin which unites the Name Yeshua to the term 'guilt offering' and to the title HaShem i.e., the Name of God.

This is stunning that such a teaching regarding the Person of Yeshu is so clearly present in the text – revealed in simple patterns and the Hebrew letter shin.

As you consider these things, please let the Holy Spirit act upon the warmth of faith within you. Let the Spirit of God act upon you quietly and joyously as you ponder His mysteries, which mysteries, in His love for you, He now brings to you attention. In particular reflect upon the teaching that God repeatedly connects His Name, Yahweh, to the Hebrew Name for Jesus, Yeshu. It seems this is the primary focus we find in Genesis 2: 7-8. The Father, blessed be He, is teaching us that He has a Son and His Name is Yeshua. In some impossible to understand fashion Yeshua and Yahweh are One Yet differentiated.

"If you have eyes to see, see!" Matt.11:15

The True Divide Between Christianity and Judaism

It's worth noting the historic divide between Judaism and Christianity does not necessarily trace its roots to a theological debate about a multiplicity of Persona within the singularity of Divinity since there were numerous historic and greatly respected proponents of this teaching within

Judaism itself. Rather, the divide revolves around the Person of Yeshua as being *'that Very One'* pointed to by our theologies. It also centers upon the perceived conclusion, 'if I am Jewish, for me to believe in Yeshua as being my Messiah, I have to become a Christian' and renounce Judaism. As we have discussed elsewhere in this book – such is definitely not the case.[81]

We can now put our differences aside. God Himself is settling the issues for us all. *Yeshua is HaShem and HaShem is teaching Torah!* We no longer have to debate questions about Who Yeshua is or is not. Our only question now should be, 'what am I going to do about what HaShem, God, is revealing?' There is an appendix at the end of this book which hopefully will address many of these questions.

Returning to Origins

At this point, we can now return to the subject of origins. Yeshua is the One pointed to by that misspelled Hebrew word vayyitser וייצר . This misspelled word led us to the pathways which we have followed so far. We have learned His originations are of different sorts. His is the origination of eternal begetting outside of time and outside of the creation; yet, His is also, paradoxically, the origination inside time and within the creation as the Righteous branch spoken of by the prophets.

> *In the beginning (origin) was the Word, and the Word was with God and the Word was God. The same was in the beginning with God. All things were made by Him: and without Him was not anything made that was made. Jn.1:1-3*

We further read in Jn.1:14, that the

> *'Word became flesh and dwelt among men'.*

---

[81] This is to say 'to become what Jews perceive to be 'anti- Jew'.

It is important to note right here, Christianity teaches that the term 'Word' in John's gospel refers to Yeshua *prior* to His advent into the creation. Simply put, the texts found at John 1:1-3, 14 teach us Yeshua is the Word of God and is God i.e., Yeshua is the incarnated express image of Divinity in that He is con-substantial i.e., of the same substance, within Divinity.

Humanity of Yeshua; God settles the Questions
Son of the Woman - Son of Mary, Miriam

The Savior incarnated into the creation and became the Human Son of the young Hebrew maid, Miriam, Mary. The literal phrase, which is revealed via an ELS count of 8^{82}, in this portion of the text is, 'boy of the breast' ילדשד. I am reminded of the verse which speaks about this, most humble aspect, of Yeshua's human nature.

> And it came to pass, as he spake these things, a certain woman of the company lifted up her voice, and said unto him, Blessed [is] the womb that bare thee, and the paps which thou hast sucked. Lk. 11:27

'Boy of the breast', what a perfect phrase. It conveys the true humanity of both Yeshua and His human mother. The word 'shad' שד[83] means among other things, 'breast' and ילד , yeleed means 'boy (of)' or 'son of'. Therefore, the

---

[82] This is the identical count which revealed the divinity of Yeshua as being the Begotten of the Father. We now see the revelations which speak of His Divine Humanity also revealed with an ELS count of eight.

שַׁד m. (b. h.; שָׁדָה, v. Ges. Thes. s. v.) *female breast.* Tosef. Sot. IV, 8 (ref. to לשד, Num. XI, 8) מה שד זה עיקר וכ' ed. Zuck. (Var. דד) as the breast is essential for the child and everything else is of secondary import, so was the

[83] manna &c.;

phrase 'yeleed shad', as we have said, translates to mean 'boy of the breast'.[84]

His human mother Miriam, though greatly favored and blessed among women was fully human none the less. Theologically, it is essential to understand that the flesh where with Yeshua was en-fleshed was that of this righteous maiden. Her flesh is exactly like the flesh of all humans. It was not exempt from sin, nor was it exempt from either hardship in labor or difficulty in life. Were this not the case, if her flesh was in some sense radically different than ours, then the flesh Yeshua took upon Himself and redeemed would likewise be different than ours and salvation would, therefore, not be possible for you or me.

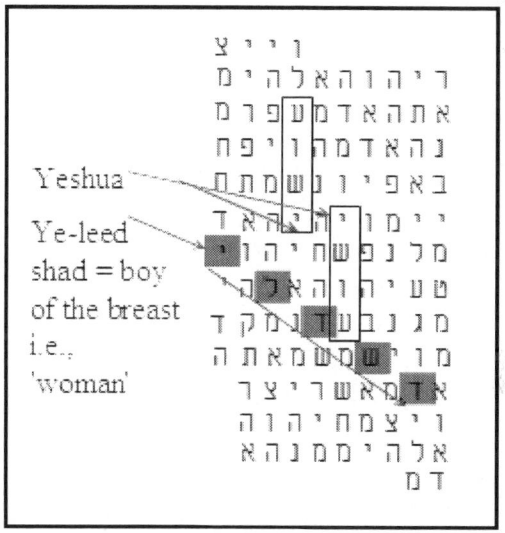

In the above illustration, the phrase 'boy of the breast' is clearly visible in the text (remember Hebrew is

---

[84] Be advised, I am aware the word shad also has a possible meaning which is, 'demon'. Considering the 'revelatory pattern' of the skip count of eight is also used in reference to Yahweh and His Begotten Son, and that the Father is God Himself, it would be blasphemy of the worst sort to adopt this demonic meaning over the meaning I have given to the term above'.

read right to left so when observing the box aligned text, begin your ELS 8 count with the letter Yud ' then skip over eight letters to the next letter, Lamed ל) etc.. Please take a moment to be certain you see this amazing revelation.

Notice how, as you count off the letters you 'overstep' the vertical spelling of the Name Yeshua and the name Miriam i.e., Mary (see above) This type of pattern is called an 'interceptive pattern' and serves to connect the elements so intercepted.   In a sense this interceptive revelation can be understood to mean, the fully Divine One was incarnated into the creation as the fully human Yeshua Who nursed His mother, Mary.. Keep in mind that we have already witnessed the revelation Yeshua is inextricably One with Yahweh Elohim, therefore, the true humanity of Yeshua, which is the subject we are now discussing, is in some – albeit, impossible to understand - fashion also One within Divinity.

Interestingly, this too is a fundamental teaching promoted in the first century by the Jewish Believers in Yeshua, the Messiah. We do not, however, see an inextricable sharing of letters between the Name Yeshua and the woman named Miriam. This is because Yeshua and the woman are not, 'one yet somehow differentiated'. Such a 'perfect' consubstantial unity is possible only within the abode which is outside time and outside the laws of physics i.e., eternity.

Recapping this Marian revelation, so far, what we see revealed is the ELS count of eight presents Yeshua as Being the Begotten of the Father united to divinity via the shared letter lamed. He is also begotten of the mother, but at the same time remains paradoxically still united to the divinity via the *same shared letter lamed.*

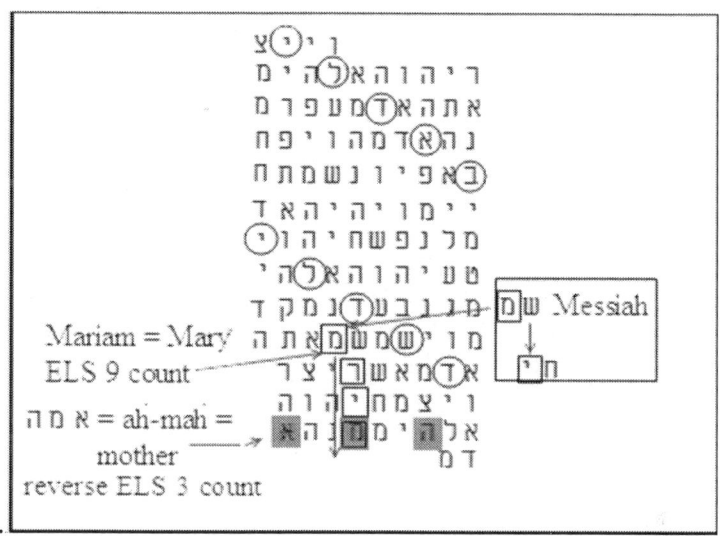

We see that Mary is His mother and hence she is the mother of the Messiah as well. The word Ah Mah means mother and it is written as a reverse ELS pattern having a three 'skip count' and serves as an interceptive pattern in our text identifying as Yeshua's. mother to be Miriam, the 'virgin' - God's 'sign' to an amazed humanity'. Obviously there is a considerable amount of Yeshuan teaching contained in this revelation – so please take time with it.

Next we see in this same remarkable revelation God's note that Yeshua is identified as the kinsman redeemer. The ELS count for kinsman redeemer is 19.

ע · · ן   Miriam = Mary
ם · ה ל א ח ו ה · ד
ם ו פ ע מ ׄ ת א ה ת א
ח פ · ו ה מ ד א ה ו
ח ח ש נ ו · ש א ב   Yeshua (the) anointed
                  (One)
ד א ה · ח · ן ם · ·
· ו ה · ח ש פ נ ד ם   גאל 'Ga-al' = kinsman
· ה ל א ח ו ה · ע ם   redeemer
ך ק מ ד ע נ נ ו ם
ה ת א ם ש מ ש · ו ם
ו צ · ה ש א מ ד א   ה ת א מ ש ו ר
ה ו ה ם ה מ צ · ·   the man 'blessed
א ה נ ם · ה א   be He'
        ם ד

In effect what is seen in this revelation is this, 'Yeshua is the kinsman redeemer, Blessed be He, the son of Mary'. This important because the Hebrew word for 'kinsman redeemer, conveys another clear Messianic reference. This word is 'ga-al' - גאל. 'Ga-al' is also displayed as an interceptive phrase in the same area of the text and appropriately connects the 'son of Mary' to the term 'kinsman redeemer'. The phrase 'kinsman redeemer' speaks to Yeshua's mission on the earth.[85] He is understood to be the One Who fully pays the price for our sin. In all, four things are required in order for a kinsman to redeem:

1. He must be near of kin (and therefore fully human) . (Leviticus 25:48; 25:25 Ruth 3:12–13)
2. He must not need redemption himself (Ruth 4:4–6).

---

[85] See Psalm 19:14, 78:35, Isaiah 41:14, 43:14, 44:6, 44:24, 47:4, 49:7, 49:26, 54:5, 54:8, 59:20, 60:16, 63:16, Jeremiah 50:34. Here the word *Goel is applied to God who is called our kinsman-redeemer.* God as redeeming man (Exodus 6:6; Isaiah 43:1; 44:22; 48:20; 49:7), and those redeemed by God (Isaiah 35:9; 51:10; Job 19:25).
Goel *(go'el)* is a Hebrew term which comes from the word *gol'el* ("to redeem")

3. He must be willing to redeem (Ruth 4:6ff)
4. He must pay the full price Redemption demanded (Leviticus 25:27; Ruth 4:7-11).

Each of these four conditions are perfectly met in the Person of Yeshua, the Son of Mary.

Yeshua Is The Lamb שה Of God

Yeshua is the God Who will become the guilt offering sacrificed on the behalf of human kind, He is our 'spotless lamb' - שה (see condition two in the discussion of kinsman redeemer above).

Our Spotless Lamb, Yeshua, is the only worthy offering because He is the only Offering directly provide by God, hence a truly perfect offering in that He does not need redemption Himself.[86] He is perfect in every way.

In Genesis 2:7-8, God reveals it is His Son, Yeshua, who becomes for us the only worthy sacrificial offering. Yeshua Alone is the only true 'spotless lamb'.

Indeed, when one considers what is being said here the only conclusion which can be drawn is that the only worthy sacrifice possible is the sacrifice which is actually provided by God himself. Doesn't it stand to reason that even the most spotless lamb, by human standards, would have some type of flaw? Perfection can originate only 'outside' the creation. It can never flow out of imperfection.

What Christians are taught regarding the person of Yeshu, however, is that Yeshu is God and therefore He is the perfect spotless lamb of God Who was provided by God as the only worthy spotless offering. They are taught that it is in the shedding of His Blood i.e., His divine blood, that the act of the atoning sacrifice is completed and fulfilled - once

---

[86] Yeshua's provision by His Father was prefigured by the provision of the ram in substitution of Isaac as the sacrificial offering by his father Abraham. This is the subject matter of another book.

and for all time. The evidence God has placed into the text, identifying Yeshua to be 'the spotless Lamb is as stunning as it is compelling. Indeed, He connects the spelling of the word sheep or lamb to the Name Yeshua six times!

ה ש =seh = lamb or sheep

In God's revelation it is exegetically impressive yet subtle that in each of the six times we see the word lamb spelled out, the word lamb begins from within the spelling of the Name Yeshu – and can be found no where else - sharing with the Name Yeshu the letter shin – the meaning of which letter we have alluded to earlier.[87] Impressive too, for the

---

[87] "The secret of the *shin* is "the flame bound to the coal [Divine Essence]." A simmering coal actually possesses an invisible flame within it, which emerges and ascends from the surface of the coal when the coal is blown upon...., the inner flame is the 'paradoxical latent presence of the power of change' within the changeless. The outer flame of the *shin* is continuously in a state of motion and change." Gal Einai Website

Jewish exegete, is the fact that the number six has the meaning of the word, 'nail'. We have already seen that the letter Vav also means 'to nail'; and, in either camp, the word 'nail' is inexorably tied, in some fashion, to the Name Yeshu. The reader might want to compare each of these six revelations of the word 'lamb' with Jesus Name, Yeshua. In so doing you will note each of these are inextricably One with the other. Yeshu is the Lamb and the Lamb is Yeshu.

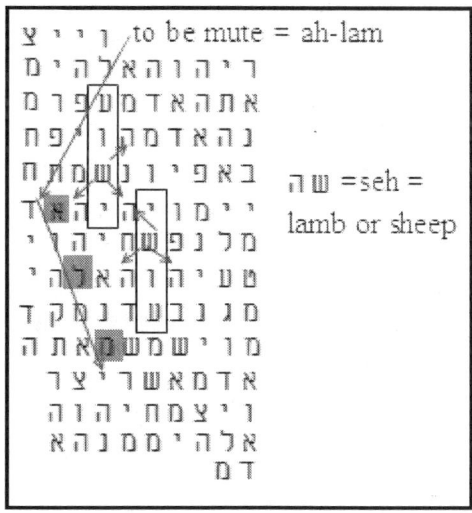

Once again, the contextual relevance of what God has encrypted into the text cannot be overlooked especially in light of the fact the word 'lamb', in each of the six times it is found, is inextricably connected with the letter 'shin' and the Person of Yeshua Who was 'nailed' to the cross on our behalf. He became for us the perfect atoning sacrifice in the spilling of His blood. He became the perfect Lamb of God sacrificed upon the same spot patriarch Abraham nearly drenched with the blood of his own son, his own only begotten son, Isaac, in obedience to the Will of God. Moreover, about this lamb we read Isaiah's prophetic words:

He was oppressed, and he was afflicted, yet he opened not his mouth: he is brought as a lamb to the slaughter, and as a sheep before her shearers is dumb, so he openeth not his mouth. Is. 53:7

In conclusion, let's focus upon two words, the Name Yeshua and the word 'asher - אשר'.[88] In Hebrew 'asher' is used as a relative participle attaching one part of a sentence to another part of the same sentence. For example in the text under consideration, we read, '... the Adam whom (asher - אשר) He formed' Gen 2:8. The word 'whom' connects both of the thoughts in this statement to each other. There are two spellings of the word 'asher' to be found in the text. One is found directly under the 'descending spelling of the Name Yeshua and forms the core of the phrase 'the blessed man' or 'the blessed be He Man'. The other is seen as a large 'x marks the spot pattern'. It forms it's junction at the letter 'shin', which letter, as said before, reveals the paradoxical latent potential for change within the changeless.

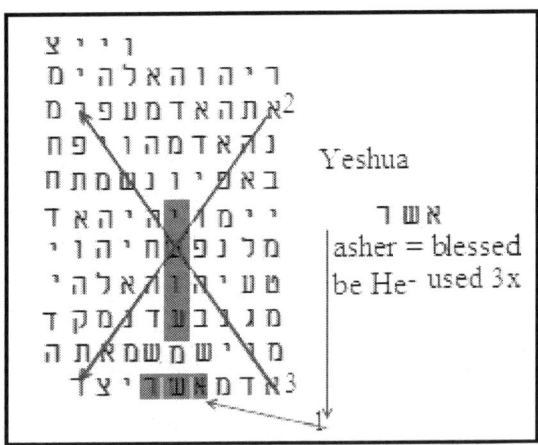

What this encryption reveals is this: Our Holy Father and Sovereign God has intentionally declared that His Son

---

[88] Asher is drawn from the Hebrew root word 'shar' which means to 'bind or tie'.

Yeshua is forever blessed (because in Hebrew grammar the 'Piel Stem'[89] of the word 'asher - אשר' conveys the meaning 'to pronounce another to be blessed').

And, to this statement we can only add, Amen!

---

[89] Piel stem usually expresses an "intensive" or "intentional" action.

Chapter 8 - So What Do I Do Now?

Yahweh said:
> *You have heard all this; look, must you not acknowledge it?*
>
> *As of now, I announce to you new things from this time, Well-guarded secrets you did not know. Only now are they created, and not of old;*
>
> *Before today you have not heard them; You cannot say, 'I knew them already'. You had never heard, you have never known, your ears were not opened of old. Is.48:6-8*

What Do I Do Now?

Your answer to this question really depends a great deal upon your willingness to believe what you have just seen with your own eyes.

Today, Yahweh Himself set before your eyes His well-guarded secrets; namely, that Yeshua and Yahweh are indeed One Divinity, yet paradoxically differentiated; and, that the Messiah, Yeshua, has already come.

For some, this message will be welcomed with great excitement and untold joy. For others, this teaching will be an unwelcome test of belief, traditions and heritage. For a few, God's revelations will produce shock, confusion and sorrow. The 'bottom line' to all this is simply, 'you still have to answer to God Himself; His question remains.

You have heard all this; look, must you not acknowledge it? Is.48:6

You are, today, invited to either 'acknowledge' what you have just seen or to turn your eyes aside and deny the revelations. Regardless of your decision, Messiah is never-the-less coming again to destroy evil, bring peace upon the earth and establish His kingdom, entering into fellowship with all who recognize His Divine Sovereignty.

> I will return to Zion and dwell in Jerusalem. Then Jerusalem will be called the *City of Truth*, and the mountain of the LORD Almighty will be called the Holy Mountain." Zech.8:3

The revelations of these *well-guarded secrets* of God give you good reason to rejoice and be glad. Today Salvation has come unto your house, 'behold the Savior stands at the door and knocks', inviting you to welcome Him into your abode. So then, if this is your situation, your next step is to 'open the door of your heart', allowing Him to enter into spiritual fellowship with you. He knocks, but you have to open. He invites fellowship, but *you* have to welcome Him.

One of the things which is so wonderful about this invitation is its simplicity. Nevertheless, there are a few things which need to be 'put into order' for you to properly respond to His invitation.

1. Put your heart and soul in order.

    The Father simply looks to you for your earnest 'desiring' to accept His Sovereignty over your life.

    > "And you will seek me and find me, when you search for me with all your heart." Jeremiah 29:13

2. Be obedient to the Father.

    Love His Begotten One, His Son, Yeshua. Accept - the Fathers teaching that in Yeshua you now have a High Priest. Yeshua has become your Mediator between Our Heavenly Father and yourself; and, that it is in Yeshua's voluntary sacrifice that He has become 'the Offer-er and the Offered'. He has become your High Priest and the 'eternally accepted sacrifice' - accepted by the Father and offered on your behalf. Accept the

107

teaching that in Yeshua, the 'dividing curtain' or 'veil' separating you from the Father is now removed.[90] All you need to do to be united with the Father is to acknowledge that Yeshua is your Redeemer, provided by the Father, to be your eternally acceptable 'blood sacrifice' – offered on your behalf – and His being the sufficient atonement for your sins. In fulfillment of what is spoken about in the Talmud[91], no longer is the temple required, you have your temple – this One is not made by human hands – it is Yeshua. No longer does an elaborate ritual need to be performed nor an animal need to be slaughtered in sacrifice to provide the blood to 'cover over' your sins – thus hiding your guilt, you now have a new sacrifice – it is the perfect Lamb – it is Yeshua, and in Him, no longer are your sins covered over and 'hidden from the sight of God' – in Him your sins are washed away! In Yeshua, your sins are 'no-more'! They are 'no more'!

If you have never done this before, why not stop and pray now:

> " Father, thank You for the great gift of Your Son, Jesus Who became my Savior and Who died for my sins and the sins of all mankind.

---

[90] History notes at the precise moment of Yeshua's death upon the altar of the cross Yeshua spoke the words traditionally spoken by the high priest in the temple when he slaughters the sacrificial lamb, i.e., "it is finished". As history reflects, at this precise moment, the Veil of Separation in the Jewish Temple was destroyed being miraculously rent in twain – from top to bottom thus-by indicating that in Yeshua's sacrifice the division between God and man is, in like manner, no more.

[91] From the Talmud:

Moses spake before the Holy One, blessed be He, "will not a time come when Israel have neither tabernacle nor temple? What will happen to these people as regards atonement?" The Holy One, blessed be He, replied, "I will take a righteous man from amongst them and make Him a pledge on their account, and I will atone for their iniquities."[91]

I treasure Him in my heart and accept Him as Your Gift. He shall be for me my God. He shall be for me my Mediator with You and through 'His blood sacrifice' I come to You as your child, washed clean from sin, restored to You forevermore".

3. Be obedient to the Fathers' Son, Yeshua.

A.   Yeshua commands us to love the Father with all our might and to love our neighbors as ourselves. He says:

'Hear, O Israel: The Lord our God, the Lord is one. Love the Lord your God with all your heart and with all your soul and with all your mind and with all your strength.' (Deut.6:4)

'The second is this: 'Love your neighbor as yourself.' (Mark 12:29-30a)   There are no commandments greater than these."– *Mark 12:30b (NIV)*

B.   Seek to fulfill the two ordinances Yeshua enjoins upon all who, in faith, will follow Him. These rituals are 'baptism and communion', i.e., the ritual of the 'mikveh' -   מִקְוֶה - and the eating of the Passover [92]– פסח

---

[92]Baptism - this ritual washing of the *Jews* is clearly evidenced in the life of the primitive Jewish Christian Church. In Jewish thought, baptism is a religious ablution signifying purification or consecration. It was also considered to be an initiatory rite and was always enjoined upon converts. The idea is that when one converts to Judaism he must do so in a condition of purity. An atonement for his past sin is required via his being sprinkled with the blood of a sacrificial offering. He would next approach the mikveh מִקְוֶה , the collection of waters - i.e., baptism - to wash off the blood with clean water. He is now considered to be, cleansed and made "whiter than snow". Cf. Ez. 36:25[92]

So too, in the Jewish Christian faith, when one seeks to enter its fellowship by accepting the blood covering of the eternal sacrifice accomplished in Yeshua. He solemnizes this event by his baptism in the

4. Know the truth. Stop the arguments.

> Guide me (us) in your truth and teach me, for you are God my Savior, and my hope is in you all day long."(Psalm 25:5)

This book does not have as its goal 'religious proselytizing'. The term proselytize implies bringing about 'conversions' to faith through the activity of convincing argumentation. What God has brought to us today requires no conversation, no argumentation. One simply needs to look – to see – to believe or - to refuse what He lays out for us to see. "The term, "religious proselytizing" [93] is most often employed to prejudice the public against efforts religious faithful use to secure conversions to their beliefs. The simple fact of 'knowing' that it is God Who is revealing

---

Mikveh. Arising from its depths, he is 'washed and made clean' – not by the water but by the blood - and enters under the shelter of the wings of the Most High.

Communion – was the core and essential ritual of primitive Christianity. Its meaning must be understood in the context of the eating of the Paschal Lamb. It was taught the consumption of the Passover i.e., the Pascal Lamb, becomes for the believer the consumption of the Body of Christ (Who was proclaimed by John the Baptist to be the 'Lamb of God'. – this was a powerful title, well understood by the Jews – its meaning is generally not appreciated by gentile audiences). To consume the Pesach is to consume the Christ. His Flesh is absorbed into the believers flesh, His Blood into the believers blood – His flesh is truly food indeed, His blood is truly drink indeed. Cf. Jn. 6:55 the word 'indeed' is in Greek ἀληθῶς $alēthōs$ and means 'of a reality', hence not a symbol but a factual thing. In this act, believers understood their unity in Yeshua; and, in this unity, they understood their unity with each other. Yeshua's body and blood is in them and their flesh is in Him. In Him they are purified and therefore they are now are made presentable before the Face of God.

[93] This term is used most frequently in Israel, becoming a common term with the passage on December 25, 1977, of Israel's infamous "anti-missionary" law. This is a statute that decrees a prison term of up to five years for any gentile attempting to proselytize a Jew away from his faith...

the revelations found in this book eliminates the need to proselytize. Our only choice is to simply accept or not accept what is now in front of our eyes. It has been said:

> When Mashiach משיח (Messiah) comes, theological truths will be *obvious* to mankind, and there will be no reason to argue about it.[94]

No, this book is not a book about 'religious proselytizing' it is not a debate about theological points or ideas. How can we even speak of proselytizing? Toward which 'religion' should new believers in Yeshua be converted? In fact, if the truth be told, we all got it wrong. Humanity has erred from its start in its attempt to define God, to ritualize God's worship and usurp God's teachings regarding human behavior and interaction. For all of these efforts, only minute benefits have resulted. In the past and in present time, religionists of every stripe have often all but abandoned the love and worship of God. Religion is today shaped by man's needs and desires. Instead of the function of religion being revealed in our blessing God and Praising His Holy Name, hungering for His Heavenly Kingdom, humanity seeks from religion a god to deliver to it the bounty of that kingdom upon the earth. Humanity builds great churches, constructs great theologies and convenes great assemblies all having the form of religion but in fact these things are little more than the 'dry bones' spoken about by Ezekiel, the prophet, so long ago. Rather than properly assembling together to seek 'first' the Will of the One True

---

[94] *http://www.jewfaq.org/mashiach.htm - Judaism101 online*

Although Messiah has already come, this citation does not refer to this fact. Instead, contextually, it applies to His future advent as the conquering king – both Jews and Christians can agree to this future application.

(*A most important aside needs to be made here. It is this. 'Since theological truths such as those you are witnessing today are amazingly being revealed and made known to us we can conclude Messiah is about to come'. ed.*)

Sovereign God, they assemble together to seek a god which accommodates their agenda, an agenda which 'effectively propounds' the teaching that mankind already knows God's Will. However, the Will which they claim to know is not God's Will at all. Rather, it is the will which says to humanity at large, 'do what thou wilt', 'believe what thou wilt'.[95]

Thus in separating themselves from the Will of the 'Very Source of Life Itself' which Will holds firmly to absolutes - to 'rights and wrongs' - they have become as dry as 'dead men's bones'. In this, we are reminded of the poignant question asked by God, "can these bones live?" Ezekiel 37:3.

Reading on, we learn, yes, the dry bones can live but only after Yahweh restores the breath of 'the way, the truth and the life', which is manifest in His Spirit, 'unto them'. Although God asks Ezekiel about the nation of Israel, '...', 'can these bones live?', His question is appropriate for us as well. It speaks to the issue of the spiritual dryness, just discussed, manifested in our 'sin weary world,' today.

Now, compare what has just been said with what the 'pattern our faith' sets for us to follow, all of us who hunger for 'pure' religion:

> Pure religion and undefiled before God and the Father is this, To visit the fatherless and widows *in their affliction*, and to keep himself unspotted from the world. James 1:27[96]

---

[95] Commandment #1 found in the satanic bible by Antone LeVey.

[96] θρησκεία καθαρὰ καὶ ἀμίαντος παρὰ τῷ θεῷ καὶ πατρὶ αὕτη ἐστίν ἐπισκέπτεσθαι ὀρφανοὺς καὶ χήρας ἐν τῇ θλίψει αὐτῶν ἄσπιλον ἑαυτὸν τηρεῖν ἀπὸ τοῦ κόσμου. In a levitical sense, in a levitical sense the word pure implies clean, the use of which is not forbidden, imparts no uncleannessfree from corrupt desire, from sin and guiltfree from every admixture of what is false, sincere genuineblameless, innocentunstained with the guilt of anything. Strongs unabridged concordance.

And thou shalt love the LORD thy God with all thine heart, and with all thy soul, and with all thy mightDeut.6:4

Thou shalt love thy neighbor as thyself. Matt.22:39 cf. Lev. 19:18

This book is about God's exhortation to us all to exhibit sincere faith in the things He is revealing to us our need to possess, heartfelt love and repentance from sin. Keep in mind, God is about to take great action in His creation. The Day of the Lord is upon us all. Conduct your lives accordingly and earnestly seek Him out in all your endeavors. Understand that He is present in all that you do.

Reveal these truths to others

Try to fellowship with other believers. *Show* to them these old yet newly re-revealed revelations which God is bringing to light today. Tell others what you now know. Study the text of scripture. Seek guidance in your study and always question what appears to be opinion or the doctrines of men. Pray and wait upon the coming of the Lord. Yahweh teaches us, 'My ways are not mans ways'. So, flee from the 'ways of men' - false piety and religiosity; cling instead to the ways of God.

Wait for Messiah's return – He will return as King.

"Remember, therefore, what you have received and heard; hold it fast, and repent. But if you do not wake up, I will come like a thief, and you will not know at what time I will come to you." Rev.3:3

"Therefore keep watch because you do not know when the owner of the house will come back — whether in the evening, or at midnight, or when the rooster crows, or at dawn. If he comes suddenly, do not let him find you sleeping. What I say to you, I say to everyone: 'Watch!'" Mk. 13:35-37

"And the Lord Shall be King over all the earth; in that day, the Lord shall be One and His Name shall be one." Zech.14:9

Concerning these matters, the consistent teaching of scripture and the revelations God is bringing into the light of day is this: wait and pray, love the brethren, adore the Father, worship the Son and remain faithful. Observe His ordinances i.e., Baptism and Communion as being your righteous obedience having their fulfillments in your unity in Yeshua through the operation of His Holy Spirit which He permits to indwell in you. Trust that God will lead your heart to where it needs to be.

The Way [97]

In the old days the followers of Jesus, the Messiah, referred to their discipleship as, 'The Way'. This was, at a time, when there were no clergy, no churches with crosses on the steeple, no hymnals, and no pomp of liturgical ritual. This was at a time when there were no complex Christian creeds, no theologies and no grandiose Christian assemblies.

Instead, this was a time when people wore sandals and their feet were covered in the dust of the roads. This was at a time when the followers of 'The Way' were Jewish, and worshipped a Jewish Messiah. The only faith related documents were 'at best' just a few handwritten letters to other followers of 'The Way' and the Hebrew scrolls of a *Jewish Bible not a New Testament*. Actually, daily life for

---

[97] This term was appended to the early followers of Jesus Who referred to Himself as 'the Way, the Truth, and the Life' thus indicating that no one comes to the Father but through Him. just as no one entered the Holy of Holies in the temple unless he had passed through it gates which were also named 'the way, the truth and the life.

believers at the start of the Yeshuan era was no different than was it for any non-messianic believer. Those who believed in the Messiah, Jesus, were Jews and were recognized as such by mainstream Judaism - a sect perhaps, but Jews nonetheless.

The 'Yeshuan' brethren still went to the synagogues, participated in the temple worship and celebrated the Jewish feasts. They still argued over the meanings attached to the texts of the 'Old Testament' (remember the New Testament was not yet written). They gathered in the houses of friends, fellowshipped and although they broke the bread of His Presence, i.e., communion; and, even this action looked 'very Jewish'. In short, Judaism did not end. Rather, via the Messianic revelation, it shifted its focus from the anticipation of the first coming of Messiah to the anticipation of His second coming i.e., His return to complete 'the age', to destroy evil and to usher into the creation His Holy Kingdom.

So, here we are today. What you are being exhorted to do is to look deep into your souls and with God's help find that inner place where you too can see yourself as a follower of 'The Way'. 'The Way' is more a matter of belief, attitude and behavior than it is of a church organization. One can follow 'The Way' in any situation of life because 'The Way' is a reflection and a reality of a heart deeply in love with God.

Among the peoples of the earth many do seek God, searching for Him with 'all their heart'. So these revelations are for them as well. 'The Way' is for them as much as it is for all of us. They have been encrypted into the text this way so that regardless of your theological stand you cannot refute what is before your eyes – Yeshua is Lord!

Bless ye the Lord all you servants of the Lord
who stand by night in the house of the Lord. The LORD bless
thee out of Zion; even He that made heaven and earth
Ps. 134:1-3

Chapter 9 – Types of Encryptions Found In This Study

ELS, Mirrored Image Encryption

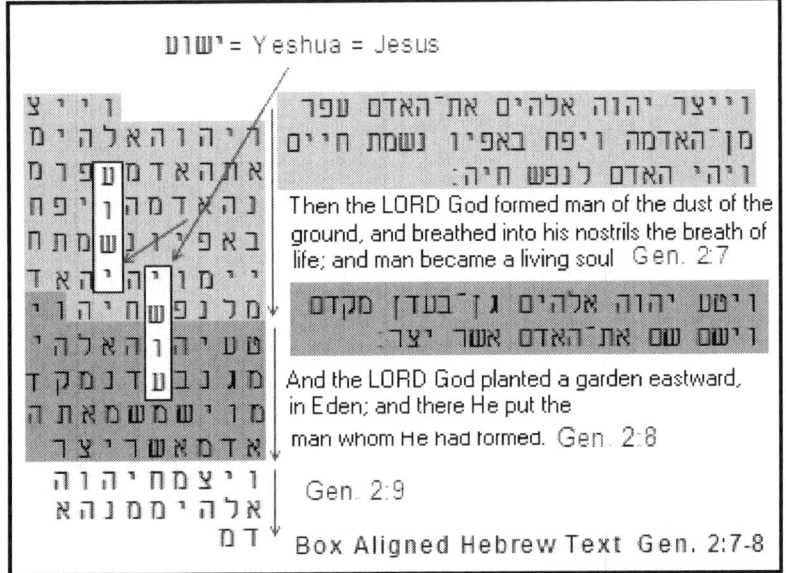

Looking at both Names Yeshua each seems to be a reflection of the other as it would appear in a mirror. Also in each case, each of the letters are equally spaced apart hence they are referred to as Equidistant letter spaced, ELS, encryption.

Inextricably Connected Patterns of Letters and Words

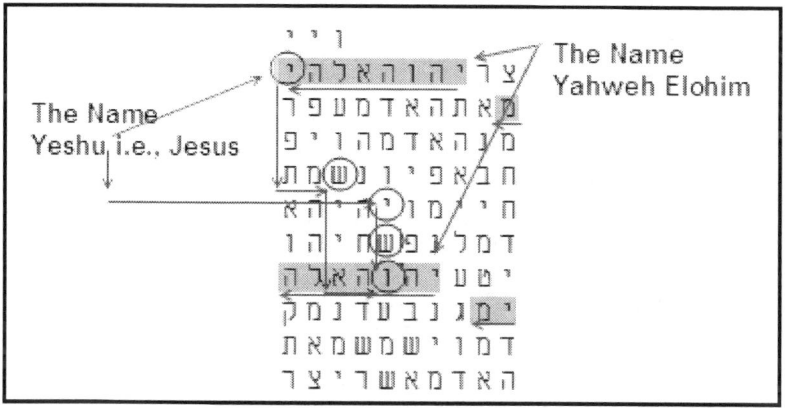

This type of pattern may have any number of words crossing each other and sharing a letter between them. In the above example, the words are the Names, Yeshua and Yahweh Elohim – the shared Hebrew letters are a yud - ' - and a vav – ו. Theologically speaking, this connotes a deep 'unity of an interactive connection' between the crossed words sharing these letters. The Names are said to be inextricably connected in that you cannot remove the shared letters from either of the Names without doing irreparable harm to the other Name which shares the same letter.

Pictogram Pattern – (discussed in chapter 4)

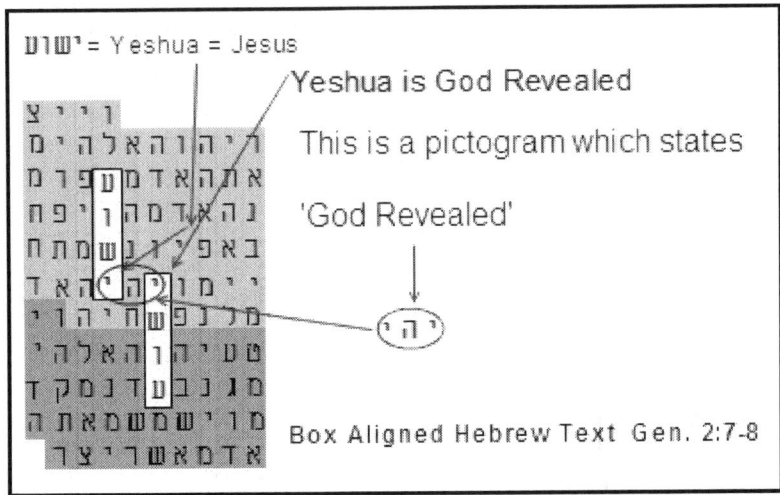

Letter sharing Pattern

The one letter being shared can form two words in this case the letter shared is the letter Hey - ה. Notice that the letters being shared are the identical letters included in the preceding illustration. In the former image, the letters represent 'pictures' while in the above, the letters are read as letters. This is an amazing revelation in that the same message is herein given in two unique ways, first as an image second as a message. I can only emphasize that God wants this message to be known.

Multiple Words From Single Word Pattern

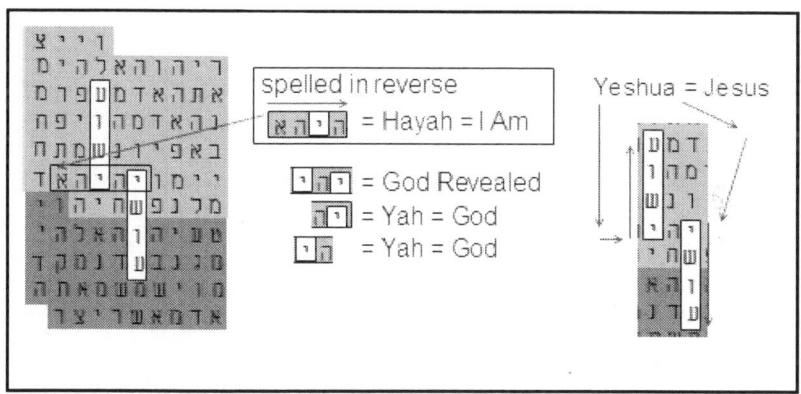

This is an excellent example of multiple words being inter woven into a single word or phrase. Consider for a moment the marvelous intricacy of the Father's thought in arranging His text this way. Each of the words listed in the illustration are inextricably connected to the Names Yeshua; and, each of these words are words which have been understood as pertaining to Yeshua. Moreover, if one were to consider only the letters which inextricable unites the title 'I Am' to both Names Yeshu he would be observing a two letters yud – ' which spells the Name Adonai – which is one of the Names for God. Also all of this is found in a text in which the faithful have always said Yeshua is the primary participant!

Simple Embedded Shape - Design Pattern

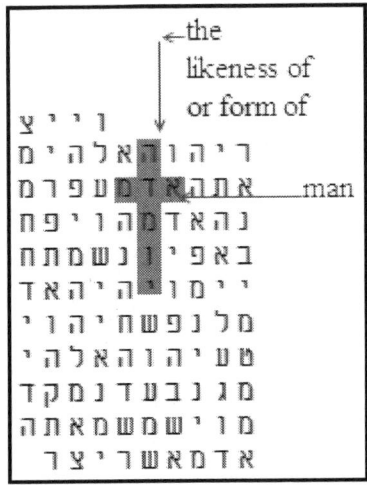

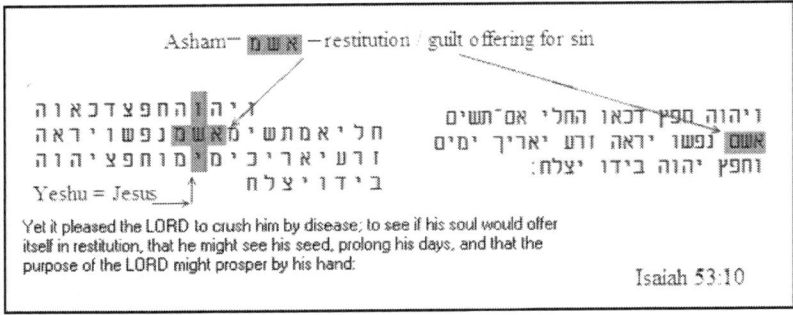

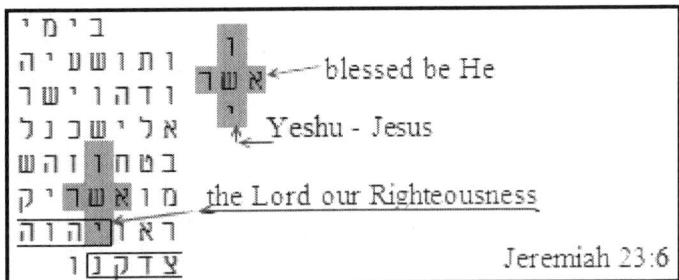

In many places in the scripture a cross can be found formed by the intersecting of the Name Yeshu and the words HaShem (a word which substitute for a Gods Name) or

Asham which means 'guilt offering' in Hebrew or the word Asher which proclaims 'blessed be He'.

Simple ELS Pattern

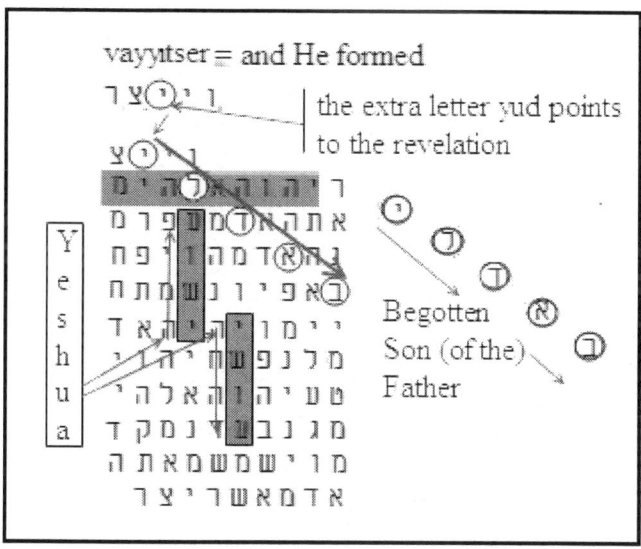

A basic eight count is the skip sequence in this pattern. It is noteworthy how other encrypted patterns are inter connected thus revealing profound teaching regarding Yeshua.

Nine By Nine Pattern Plus A Design Encryption

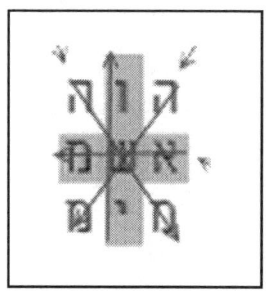

This pattern is repeated in several places in the scripture. See the illustration for Isaiah 53:10 above. Each of the words formed in this pattern directly relay to Jesus, Yeshua, also the cross is contextually correct and relates to Him as well. Asham אשמ = guilt offering, Yeshu ישו = Jesus Name, HaShem השמ = a special Name of God. The cross is self explanatory.

Small X Marks The Spot Pattern

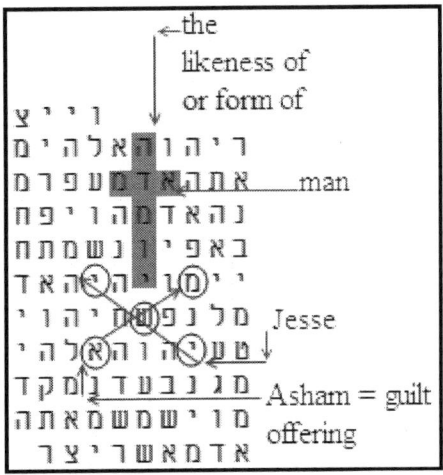

Combination ELS / Repeating Mirrored Image Pattern

The word Asham or 'guilt offering' appears twice while the ELS is inextricably connected To the Name Yeshua.

Large X Marks The Spot Pattern

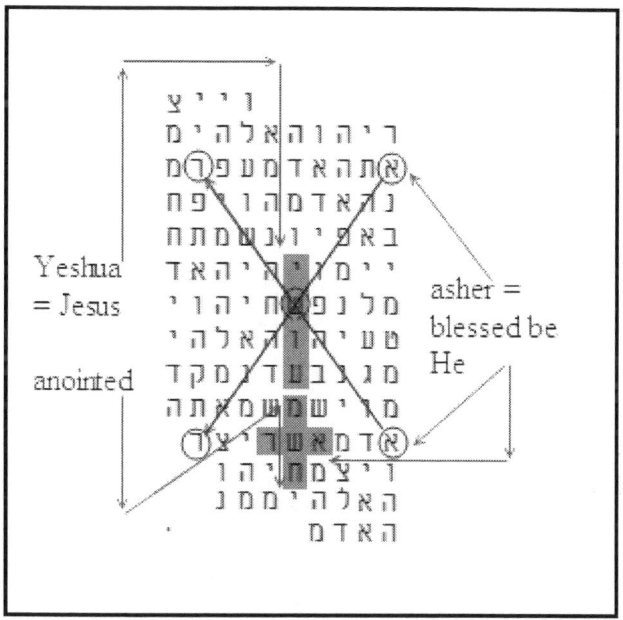

The pattern is formed by two long ELS pattern legs criss crossing over each other at the letter shin – they spell asher, 'blessed be He' and each leg is pinned to the Hebrew Name of Jesus.

Also note the image pattern encryption of a cross which incorporates the same word i.e., asher inextricably connected to the word 'anointed'.

Contained in this illustration is the three fold repetition 'blessed be He', 'blessed be He', 'blessed be He' - with each repetition of the phrase 'blessed be He' appended to the phrase 'the anointed Yeshua'

Connective Phrase Pattern

```
ע י י ו
ם י ה ל א ה ו ה י ר
ם י פ ד ע מ ד ה ת א
ח פ י ו מ ד א ה נ
ח ת מ ש י נ ו ו א פ ב
ד א ה י ה י מ י ו א ר ת
י ו ה י ח פ נ ל מ
י ה ל א ה ו ה י ע ט
ד ק מ נ ד ב ע נ ג נ מ
ה ש ש מ ת א ש ו י מ
ר צ י ד ר ש א מ ד א
ה ו ה י ח מ צ י ו
א ה נ מ מ י ה ל א
ד מ
```

הש =seh = lamb or sheep

The word seh i.e., lamb is found six times, each time it appears it connects the Names Yahweh and Yeshua.

Repeated Sequence Patterns

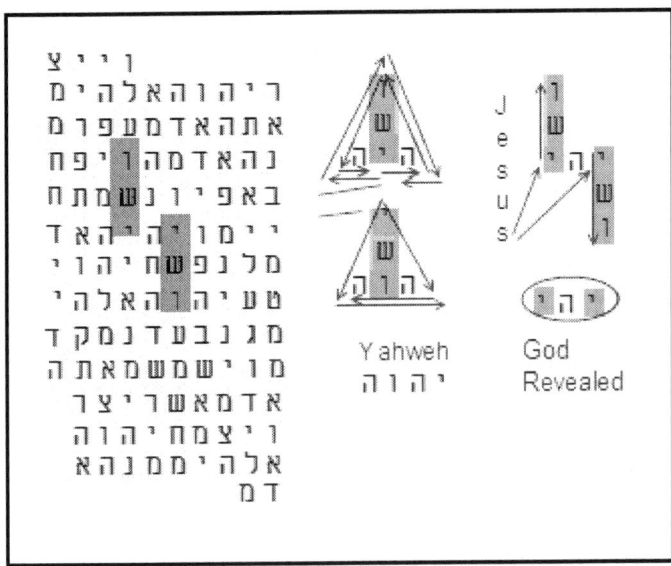

Obviously this type of pattern can only be called a pattern in that it repeats itself within the boundaries of the text being studied. If this were not the case, any combination of any letters spelling names and phrases could be possible. A bible code program would never pick up this kind of pattern since the letters of interest are not equidistance sequenced.

A Final Piece of Data:

Here is a simple depiction of each of the letters incorporated in the formation of the various Christological revelations found in this book. Their *exact placement in the box aligned text matrix grid* **by chance alone** represents a probability of 22 to the 70th power against!

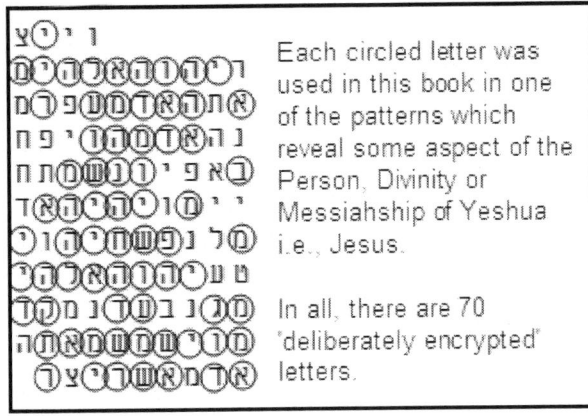

Each circled letter was used in this book in one of the patterns which reveal some aspect of the Person, Divinity or Messiahship of Yeshua i.e., Jesus.

In all, there are 70 'deliberately encrypted' letters.

Epilogue

This book began with the question:

Why would God Who dictated His scripture to His servant Moses 'letter by painstaking letter'[98], do so in such a way, that with nothing more than a simple 'box alignment' of the text, core Christian doctrines including the name Yeshua - ישוע, Jesus, instantly become clearly visible, almost jumping right off the page in the sight of even the most skeptical observer?

The answer to this question is obvious. God blessed us all with such an abundance of contextually relevant encryptions and relevant texts so that there will remain zero doubt in any person's mind that what they are witnessing in this book is nothing less than Revelations coming directly from God Himself!

In these revelations the Holy One, has Himself, *indisputably proven even to the most calloused skeptic* that He is God and that He has an eternal Son, Yeshua the Messiah.

A Personal Observation

I wonder, if the reader has ever said, "if only God would give me a sign, then I'd believe"? The point is this; humanity has always looked for signs. Sometimes God provided them. Sometimes they were wonderful. Sometimes they were not so wonderful in that they were fulfillments of His chastisements.

This book is God's sign to you.
The Day of the Lord is, at last, at Hand.

---

[98] Jewish teaching asserts God dictated this text to Moses 'letter by painstaking letter'

You have heard all this; look, must you not acknowledge it? Is. 48

Faith in things unseen is no longer the issue. The issue is, 'what action should you take based upon the things you have just seen revealed'? Now this is a most serious matter for all of us. Yahweh, God, has given the sign so frequently asked for. He has given it to us all.

God is taking all of us to task. God foreknew He would have to settle these matters for us because we would never settle them ourselves! He did this because time is running out! These last days are drawing to a close.

And like a loving Father, He is now assembling all of us - Jew, Muslim, Christian, atheist and all the rest of humanity into His Presence – people of faith and people without faith. He is saying to us all, 'will you now believe – will you now revere My Son, Yeshua – will you now come to faith'?

The answers to these questions are of course up to you, but make no mistake, it is *The One True God* Who Is asking these things. Hence our answers will seal our eternal destiny.

Judgment is upon us all. Judgment has come down upon the earth. These revelations are being brought out now because He is about to act.

In effect He is repeating for us today that familiar theme from the days of the patriarchs.

That the nations will know, I Am the God of Abraham, Isaac and Jacob

Appendix i

Not Bible Codes

Certainly, by now, you have already visually scanned or flipped through this book; and, you have glanced at the profusion of diagrams which seem to resemble Bible codes. But, resemblances can be deceiving. First of all, a Bible Code program will not produce the text/column layouts of Genesis 2:7-8 being appended to the layout of verse 9 which you have seen in this book.

Also, there are also enormous differences between God's embedded teachings and what is being offered to the public as Bible Codes. Because these differences are so great, I will not even use the term 'Bible Code' when referring to the revelations contained in this book.

This is because God Himself is supplying the revelations!

Our study is about *God Alone* and these revelations are indeed about *God*; His Nature and His Being. They come to us as patterns encrypted into the text. Sometimes they are simple ELS patterns, sometimes they are oddly shaped patterns of letters which repeat themselves and sometimes the patterns produce a design. What they all have in common is this, they all reveal *God*, His Holy Will and His ineffable interaction with his creature within the arena of His creation. His revelations clarify our human understanding about Who 'He Is' and What He wants us to know about Him and His great gift to humankind, His Messiah.

Differences

As I see it, the differences between this study and the so called 'Bible Codes' are as follows:

1. Computers are not needed. Our study does not *require* computers to locate God's secrets, His revelations, embedded in the scriptures – we may use computers from time to time - but they are not essential to our work; whereas, Bible coders are absolutely dependent upon computers.

2. We make no attempt to predict the future - i.e., practice divination; whereas, Bible coder research is *primarily focused upon and driven by the hope of 'predicting the future'.*

3. We are faithful to Biblical context. God's revelations are razor sharp and entirely contained within a few verses of text and *are fully harmonious with the context of the text being analyzed;* whereas, Bible Coders place little importance upon congruency between their findings and the text in which they are found. Their 'results' often span several books of the bible.

Computers Are Not Needed

Surprising to most Bible Code enthusiasts is the fact that Jewish Sages and Rabbis have been 'searching' the text of the Bible for 'God's embedded revelations' for millennia *and, this they have done, without computers!* Computers were not needed in the past nor are they needed today. God's revelations have always been there for anyone in any age to discover.

Two such contemporary 'non-computerized' researchers are Yacov Rambsel and Joel Young. I owe a debt of gratitude to both these men for their outstanding work[99]. They, following the traditional methods of Torah study (bequeathed to them by their own teachers) have each painstakingly hand counted millions of Hebrew letters in the

---

[99] their books are included in our bibliography

original texts looking for any 'letter skip patterns', called ELS,[100] which emerge. Their efforts have most assuredly paid off. We are all blessed by the great treasure of spiritual jewels which these faithful men have uncovered, God's Own revelations, 'embedded' in God's Word.

Our unworthy effort in this work simply adds to the enormous corpus of their research. The reader is cautioned to be ever mindful that is God Who is the 'true Author' of these wonderful revelations. It is God who embedded them into the surface text of the Bible; and if it weren't for the guidance of the Holy Spirit of God, I would not know where to look to find them or what to say about them. God Himself is the true author of this book.

Box Aligned Texts

Unique to this work is the employment of 'boxed aligned texts'. Box aligned texts physically resemble those 'word jumble puzzles' found in newspapers everywhere.

In this study, however, it quickly becomes obvious the boxed aligned texts we are viewing are much more than word jumbles. Indeed, they indisputably serve to reveal God's many, many encrypted revelations. Not only do they reveal the ELS encryptions in the Bible, but, other types of encryptions as well, i.e., Hebraic letters pictographs, non-evenly spaced patterns and patterns which take on various shapes such as a cross etc. God speaks to us in many ways, a burning bush which is not consumed, thunders, a still small voice, a dove, writings upon the wall or even as He is doing

---

[100] ELS refers to a pattern of letters deliberately inserted into a text. Referred to by the phrase equal-distance letter sequencing., cryptologists have used ELS for centuries. An example of ELS is this sentence. Note the bold letters - **R**ips **e**xplained **t**hat **e**ach **c**ode is a **c**ase **of** adding **e**very fifth or tenth or fiftieth letter to form a word. To unravel the meaning of this simple ELS cryptogram begin with letter 1, the R, then take every 4th letter in this sentence from left to right and it spells 'Read the code'. (source unknown). This is a skip pattern of 4 letters.

here – in text displayed as encrypted patterns embedded in the Bible.

The box aligned texts we are viewing allow for multiple patterns to be revealed 'all at once'. In this, they present 'God's concise dogmatic revelations' in such a manner that the reader is stunned by their *pointedness* and *congruence* with the text being studied. 'The Box Aligned Text' arrangement of scriptural passages which are 'in-context' with the revelation being presented is the 'missing link' which pulls it all together. It offers to the reader a totally new way to read scripture, rather, to observe scripture. Moreover, the use of box text alignment does not now, nor did it ever, require the employ of a computer to analyze its content and was certainly within the 'hand written scribal abilities' of the ancient Jewish scholars.

No Attempt To Predict The Future

The most important difference between this work and the Bible coders 'findings' has to do with the very *allure* touted by the Bible Codes enthusiasts themselves; namely, they promise the possibility of predicting *all future events* by using computers to locate the ELS patterns in the Bible.

The problem with their efforts is clearly spelled out in the Old Testament[101] itself. The Old Testament refers to 'future telling' as being the practice of 'divination'; and, this practice is absolutely forbidden by God.

The Hebrew word for divination is מקסם 'miqcam', meaning, to practice divination or divine the future. This word shares the same root with the word witchcraft קסם 'qecem'., hence 'future telling', divination, is at it's very root connected to the practice of 'witchcraft'. Concerning witches God's word is clear:

"Thou shalt not suffer a witch to live." Exd. 22:18.

also,

---

[101] Tanach- תנך - in Hebrew

"There shall not be found among you [any one] ...,
that useth divination, [or] is an observer of times, or
an enchanter, or a witch". Dt. 18:10

Sadly, the coders also compound their 'sin' by
crediting God with their forbidden discoveries. About this
God is also clear:

"Have ye not seen a vain vision, and have ye not
spoken a lying 'divination', whereas ye say, The
Lord saith [it]; albeit I have not spoken"? Ezek. 13:7

"But the prophet, which shall presume to speak a
word in My Name, which I have not commanded him
to speak..., even that prophet shall die". Dt. 18:20

It's particularly unfortunate that people who are
otherwise strong in their faith have fallen so deeply into the
sin of divination. Perhaps, blind to the nature of their
wrongdoing and satan's cunning devices, the coders assume
God wants us to use the very letters of the Holy Bible to
practice this sort of 'future telling'. They fail to understand
that His Holy Things, His Holy Letters and His Holy Words
used this way in the performance of these forbidden
activities, is a most abominable blasphemy.

Faithfulness To The Biblical Context
Traditional biblical exegesis[102] demands faithfulness
to the text being studied in regard to contextual relevancy.

---

[102] Exegesis (from the Greek ἐξηγεῖσθαι 'to lead out') is a critical
explanation or interpretation of a text. Biblical exegesis is a critical
explanation or interpretation of the Bible. The goal of Biblical exegesis is
to find the meaning of the text which then leads to discovering its
significance or relevance. Wiki. June 23, 2009, exegesis.

This means, that for any and every scriptural passage studied, traditional biblical exegesis demands every comment, analogy and application which the student develops must, in some fashion, be directly *relevant* to the text read. If it does not *relate* it fails the traditional, and modern, tests for proper exegesis. So highly developed is this concept in Jewish scholasticism that the Jews have, over time, developed and systematized four levels of biblical exegesis with each sequential level deepening the students understanding of the *relevancy, application and spiritual implications* of the passage being read. In short, every passage read can only be interpreted within some framework of congruent and contextual meaning.

The coders, however, place zero importance upon 'relevancy' and 'congruency'. They simply use the Bible as a data base, in this case, as a massive collection of letters – one letter next to another letter. They have little interest in context instead they look only for ELS patterns which emerge from the data base. Their findings therefore have *zero* scriptural context. In this regard the only patterns which they can locate are ELS patterns – *and computers are definitely needed for this task.* Consider for a moment, how difficult it would be to track down an ELS pattern having a skip sequence of say, 1142 letters. Without a computer it's an impossible task! The letters patterns they work with can be as tightly packed as a two letter skip or as far apart as many thousands of letters between each 'next letter' found. One letter can be found in Genesis the next in Job perhaps the next in one of the Minor Prophets. Relevancy and congruency to 'a particular passage' is impossible when the text is handled like this. A common and supportable objection often levied against the Bible Coders is 'ELS patterns can be easily found within any book containing a large quantity of letters. To this day, this critique has not be successfully overcome.

Such is not the case with the revelations God is presenting to us today. In the revelations contained in this book, we see absolute congruency to the Biblical text i.e., each of God's revelations which we discuss are found within, and are contextually relevant with, the very biblical text in which they are found. It is precisely this 'tight and razor sharp' congruency with the text that takes the revelations we discuss herein out of the realm of mere coincidence into the hard cold world of 'factual information'. This idea is further developed in the next chapter.

Method Of Study

As I went through this study I employed various 'rabbinic methods' of exegesis. I was, in particular, very attentive to the relevancy and congruency of the text. I also drew upon Christian hermeneutics[103] to expand upon these discoveries and to draw conclusions which are understandable and in line with the context of the passage being read. I'd like to caution the reader, however, that regardless of the method of exegesis I used at any given time to always remember that the method I selected to use is exactly this…, it is a method which I am employing i.e., it is *my* method of choice. *My* exegetical method as well as *my* *opinion*; and, I can be incorrect and I am often incorrect in any variety of things. Please, always keep in this mind, 'what I have to say about a revelation ought never to supersede the revelation itself'.

All that is important is the revelation itself.

If you have a complaint about my exegesis please do not hold it against the revelation. God's Revelation stands on its own – I am but a middleman – and a sinful one at that. What you have witnessed is the Newly Revealed teaching of God and I'd like the reader to keep this in mind especially as

---

[103] Hermeneutics refers to the method of interpretation used to understand a passage… usually a passage of scripture.

I plod along attempting to 'exegete the impossible to exegete', the Sublime, the Most Holy Word of our Father.

In conclusion, God's guarded teachings, which are deeply embedded into the text, are pure revelations and should not be confused with Bible codes. God's revelations are clear, razor sharp and relevant to the very passage being read.

In comparison, the Bible Codes computer programs are not designed to produce findings relevant to any topic or passage in the Bible. Also, coders 'findings' usually require *generous interpretation* to be understood. Sometimes they are downright obscure.

But, what can be said about the very, very, few but much propagandized so called 'accurate Bible Coder prophesies'? We can't say too much except, 'beware'. The reader will quickly see that such 'accurate findings' are truly of a different sort of character than are God's revelations which are contained in this book. They lack all contextual congruency and spring forth from a spirit which desires to use the Holy Bible as some sort Ouija board or crystal ball in an effort to practice occult divination, a practice forbidden by God.

Satan has, in the efforts of the 'bible coders', found a way to imitate and to twist the very word of God. Satan throws a 'Red Herring' into the works (see appendix ii and the discussion on Red Herrings). This pernicious activity is nothing new to most of us. The evil one imitates love - offering lust instead, joy finds its imitation in pleasure and righteousness in prudery. All of these substitutions are nothing more than 'Red Herrings'. In the case of the Bible Codes, that feared and wretched, enemy of humankind has drawn many well intentioned people into his net diverting even the people of God off 'the track' - from the safe pathway home to their heavenly Father. He has drawn them into the net of endless speculations concerning future events - thus occupying their time and preventing them from finding the 'true pearls' which are in fact contained in the scripture.

Finally, the very intent of Bible coders, i.e., to use the letters of the Bible to predict the future, countermands the clear teachings of the Bible itself and blasphemes God and desecrates His Book. Before being swayed by such things, one should consider that the distinguishing characteristic of a false prophet is that his prophecy fails to happen. At this writing, hundreds of key 'coder prophecies' have failed. For example, the Battle of Armageddon has not happened – though often predicted - the start and end of WWIII via atomic holocaust failed many, many, times and for many prophesized dates and Hilary Clinton being elected to the presidency of the US, although predicted by 'bible coders', was clearly a non-event.[104]

God's Encrypted Revelations Never Fail

In contrast, God's encrypted revelations never fail. Gods encrypted revelations point to real events, expounding them and clarifying their meanings. The reader will see, time after time, as each box aligned text is 'unwrapped' that *'theologically recognizable teaching'* is being affirmed, most of which teaching is probably already known to the reader.

Depending if the reader is Jewish or Christian, he may or may not be challenged by what he sees revealed; but more than likely, he will not say, 'I have never heard of such things'. Again, the revelations are not new. What the teachings say is not different *content wise* than what has been taught before.

What is different is this: 'the content of these revelations have previously been understood to be issues of theological debate. But now, the debate is over. The teachings are now being clearly spelled out in the text of scripture'. In a real sense it is God Himself Who is conducting a Bible study with us all. These teachings do not fail because they point to real events, real people and real doctrine – real history. Who can deny that they affirm the

---

[104] The Bible Codes II

clear teachings which have always been taught in all places over the course of Christian history? The revelations only leave room for us to make a choice.

The Choice

The reader can either accept that the revelations have been inserted into the text by the Hand of God or reject the idea that God had anything to with it.

Notice, I did not say the reader can refuse to accept them as being there. The revelations are there! Nor can the reader suggest they revelations are in the text by coincidence alone. There is no debate on this issue either. The science of statistics probabilities has settled this question forever. Nor can it be asserted the revelations have been inserted into the text 'after the fact'. The texts discussed herein precede 'the fact of Yeshua's Presence' by many thousands of years; and, more than enough evidence proves the text itself has changed but very little over that vast time period!

The real issue is one of choice resulting in action. This choice will require the reader to determine what he or she is going to do with what is now revealed in the Bible.

Again, regardless if the reader is Jewish, Muslim or Christian, he will probably not say, 'I have never heard of such things'. Most Jews, Muslims and Christians do know that the ancient and modern followers of Jesus affirm He is God and became Man. They know the Yeshuan faith teaches that Jesus was crucified on our behalf as a sin offering, paying the wages of sin in our stead.

Apparently the purpose behind the encryptions is to affirm these aforementioned things. They affirm what has always been taught by the ancient Jewish followers of Messiah, Yeshua. The reader is challenged to determine if he or she accepts the fact that God Himself is the 'encryptor' Who overlaid these astounding revelations across the storyline of the text. The reader is challenged to read this text with an open mind and heart. Above all else, the reader is further challenged to not reject Him by rejecting these teachings because indeed, these are His gifts to us today.

Appendix ii
Is the Hebrew Name For 'Jesus'
Yeshua ישוע or Yeshu ישו?

In recent years the question over the Hebrew spelling of the Name we refer to in English as 'Jesus' has provoked a great amount of discord in Messianic Christian circles. This spelling problem has both a historic and more contemporary context. More important however, is the fact that *this issue is really a non – issue* and exists primarily due to the agitation of anti-Christian apologists within the Jewish communities. It has become what has been termed in political circles as a 'red herring'.

A 'red herring' is anything which can distract the conversation away from the real points an opponent might be trying to make. According to Wikipedia under the heading of 'red herring', we read:

> "'**Red Herring**' is an idiomatic expression referring to the rhetorical or literary tactic of diverting attention away from an item of significance. For example, in mystery fiction, where the identity of a criminal is being sought, an innocent party may be purposefully cast in a guilty light by the author through the employment of false emphasis, deceptive clues, 'loaded' words or other descriptive tricks of the trade. The reader's suspicions are thus misdirected, allowing the true culprit to go (temporarily at least) undetected"

Once distracted, the conversation turns from the subject at hand and the day is won by the opposition. Unfortunately the discussion turns all too often from the question, 'is Yeshua the Messiah of Israel?' to, 'is Jesus' Name Yeshu or Yeshua?'

All the opposition needs to do to distract the conversation is to state something like, 'oh, you're a follower of Yeshu.' (Now, the name Yeshu is disliked in Messianic Christian circles.) The Messianic believer almost instantly reacts and corrects his opponent saying, 'no, I am a follower of Yeshua.' Before too much time elapses the conversation takes off on a different track altogether.

The disdain Messianic believers have regarding this Name needs to be re-considered. Here is why.

It is a fact that after the crucifixion of Jesus, Messianic Jewish believers did not quibble over the popular use of the names Yeshua or Yeshu. As antagonism quickly arose between the Messianic Jewish community and the non-Messianic Jewish community, the anti-Messianics did what they could to discourage the missionary activities of the Messianic Jews. Their efforts included a plethora of disparaging teachings which incorporated both Names but in particular it focused upon the Name Yeshu. The anti-missionaries concocted a vial acronym[105] for the Name Yeshu which the followers of Jesus would obviously emphatically oppose. Over time, Jewish Messianics

---

[105] The acronym essentially states the curse ''may his name be blotted out'. The following is NOT the acronym just mentioned but is an illustration how an acronym functions. The statement Jesus of Nazareth King of the Jews was written upon a plaque nailed above the head of Jesus when He was crucified. The Pharisees violently objected to Pilate , the Roman governor when they realized that the first letter in each word (the acronym) spelled out the very teaching they were trying to suppress, namely, Yeshua is Divine, Yahweh.

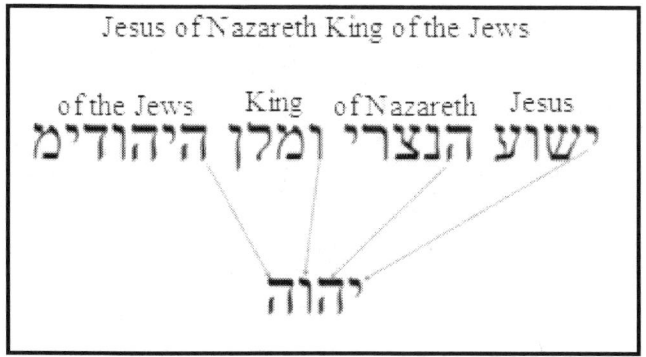

distanced themselves from using the Name Yeshu and the practice to reject the Name Yeshu took hold and is today seldom questioned but quickly accepted by Jewish and Gentile converts alike. The end result of this practice produces comments today such as, 'the use of the Name Yeshu to refer to Messiah is at best semi-blasphemous'.

Truly this is a sad state of affairs. The Name Yeshu is a perfectly good Name and the reluctance of Messianics to use it is a capitulation to the anti-Christian apologists who have hijacked the Name and deprived all of us of its place in our lives. Sadly this capitulation is due to an erroneous but deliberate false teaching regarding the Name.

The fact is, Hebrew is a versatile language and contains many spelling variants for the same words. Most notably are the variations on the spelling of the most exalted Name of Yahweh, God. They are: יהוה, יהו, יה and י. None of these spellings are considered to be diminutions of the Divine Name nor is one spelling a more 'familiar or patronizing' way of spelling the Name than are the other spellings. They each are understood to refer to the Divine Being in the exact same way and are each treated with the same measure of reverence by the reader when encountered in the Biblical text.

The same situation exists regarding the Hebrew spellings of the Name Jesus. Be He called Yeshua or Yeshu, the reference is to the same Person.

Extensive information regarding the etymology of the Name Yeshua is to be found on the website Wikipedia and the reader is urged to do a thorough study on this subject before he, without question, objects to the Name God Himself encrypted into the text of the scriptures.

God clearly identifies the Names Yeshu and Yeshua with the Person of Messiah. Obviously the Author of Genesis 2:7-8 has no problem honoring this Name, appending to it the various attributes which belong to our Savior Alone.

In each of the books to follow in the series, 'Again, God Speaks', the reader will repeatedly see the importance of the Name Yeshu validated by the fact that God Himself has encrypted it into the texts of scripture so very many times, each time connecting to it hundreds of pro-Yeshuan teachings.

To ignore such revelations which clearly point to Yeshu as being God, the Son and Messiah of Israel, is not only incorrect but it would seem to be arrogant, quite disrespectful and it would probably be blasphemous to Our most Holy and Sovereign God Who has so greatly honored this Name in His text.

So as you consider these things be mindful it is God Who placed these things into the text; and, because this is so, receive them joyfully into your heart. Honor what He honors; and, never again be reluctant to use the Name Yeshu, calling upon it with faith and love.

Bibliography

The Gospel In Ancient Hebrew, Frank T. Seekins, Ph.D. – 1996. Frank T. Seekins.

The Torah Rabbas, John F. Boylan, M. Div., ed. - 2007. LuLu Press.

The Legends of the Jews, Vol. 1, Louis Ginzberg, John F. Boylan, M. Div. ed., – 2007, Orthodox Press.

The Legends of the Jews, Vol. 2, Louis Ginzberg, John F. Boylan, M. Div. ed.,– 2007, Orthodox Press.

Behold Yeshua, Come and See!, Joel Young, D.C., 1996-1997.

Encyclopedia Judaica, Macmillan Reference USA; 2 edition (December 12, 2006). ISBN-10: 0028659287

Wikipedia.com

Blue Letter Bible.com

Made in the USA
Lexington, KY
13 January 2016